in

D0006353

RANDOM HOUSE STUDIES IN SOCIOLOGY

Consulting Editor: CHARLES H. PAGE
UNIVERSITY OF MASSACHUSETTS

Bureaucracy in Modern Society

SECOND EDITION

Peter M. Blau COLUMBIA UNIVERSITY

Marshall W. Meyer CORNELL UNIVERSITY

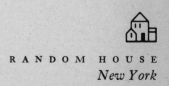

RANDOM HOUSE
New York

ISBN: 0-394-31452-2

Library of Congress Catalog Card Number: 73–156338

Manufactured in the United States of America.
Composed by H. Wolff Book Mfg. Co., Inc., New York, N.Y.

Second Edition

98765432

Foreword

In 1956, I was privileged to write the Foreword for the first edition of Peter Blau's *Bureaucracy in Modern Society*, referring to the study as "the first systematic sociological textbook on bureaucracy as such." Since then the investigation of formal organizations and the testing, modification, and elaboration of organizational theory have become a major component of the sociological enterprise, a development in which Professor Blau's works—including *The Dynamics of Bureaucracy* (1955, revised 1963), *Formal Organizations* (with W. Richard Scott, 1962), and *The Structure of Organizations* (with Richard A. Schoenherr, 1971)—have played a leading role. This development has been marked by extensive research and the publication of innumerable articles and monographs, by curricular innovations in both undergraduate and graduate programs (what department does not offer at least one course on "formal organizations"?), by the restructuring of older specializations such as "industrial sociology," and, of course, by the appearance of a large number of textbooks and anthologies (there was only one such collection in the 1950s). During the last fifteen years or so, the subject of "bureaucracy" has been worked and reworked by sociologists and other social scientists and has become a frequent theme of journalism, fiction, and "popular sociology"; the pioneer writings of Max Weber and Robert Michels have been widely studied and, especially in Weber's case, have been reevaluated and sometimes sharply criticized; what were once largely fugitive materials are now assembled between hard and soft covers; and the subject occupies a central position in the ongoing radical critique of the social order.

With all of this, one might expect a "short study" (118 pages) on this large and crucial subject to have become obscured. That *Bureaucracy in Modern Society* has suffered no such fate is attested by its continuing use in many schools and in a variety of courses in sociology, by its adoption for courses in other disciplines (for example, government, economics, and education), and by its translation into at least six languages. The widespread and persistent use of this book, surely, stems from its several merits, described in part in the earlier Foreword as "theoretical sophistication and conceptual precision; skillful and illuminating utilization of concrete materials . . . ; clarity of exposition, free of unnecessary jargon and designed to hold the reader to the march of the analysis; economy of presentation, encouraging the student to read more widely in the field. . . ." These virtues remain as important features of this expanded edition of the study by Professors Blau and Marshall W. Meyer.

The revision provides students and teachers with new, additional riches. For example: Chapter 3 on "Bureaucracy in Process" includes a provocative discussion of bureaucratic ideologies, in which the positive and negative functions of "glorifying myths" and "the myth of scientific management" are brought out sharply, an analysis that makes effective use of recent work by such scholars as Philip Selznick and Wilbert Moore. Chapter 4 on "Bureaucratic Authority" presents an insightful treatment of the role of expertness with respect to *both* authority and power, based in part on the important studies of Victor A. Thompson and Michael Crozier; and the same chapter concludes with a cogent "note on collegiality," an overly neglected feature of many present-day organizations. Chapter 5, a major addition and in keeping with a current (and long overdue) trend, concerns "The Comparative Study of Organizations," both cross-culturally and cross-organizationally: the principal dimensions and methods of comparative analysis, and the advantages and limitations of case studies, are clearly depicted; and significant findings by Arthur Stinchcombe, Stanley Udy, and Marshall Meyer, among others, are used to support the merits—and potentialities—of comparative study. In Chapter 6 on "Bureaucracy and Social Change," a sturdy carry-over from the earlier edition, the analysis of "conservative pressures," anchored in graphic case studies, has been updated and enriched by a revealing portrayal of the unwon war on poverty. "The Transformation of Bureaucracy" itself is dealt with in the new Chapter 7, which includes, in addition to a developed discussion of the problematics of "efficiency" (some of which are vividly illustrated in a caveat on the Vietnam War), a timely treatment of the impact of modern technology on the nature of work and on organizational structure, as shown by recent investigations including those of Robert Blauner in this country and of Joan Woodward and others in Britain. The concluding chapter on "Bureaucracy and Democracy" incorporates a report of Stanley Milgram's now-famous experiment in obedience; overcompliance with authority, as Blau and Meyer point out, has important implications for governmental policy and practice and, more generally, for political democracy.

This study as a whole, it should be stressed, teaches important lessons about what often seems to be the paradoxical role of bureaucracy in contemporary society. On the one hand, it underscores the inescapable fact that the achievement of myriad goals—the production of needed goods, the provision of needed services, the education of young and old, the political enlistment of a huge citizenry, the maintenance of equity and justice, the pursuit of reformistic or revolutionary aims, the protection of the environment, the attainment indeed of "antibureaucratic" decentralization—demands *organization*. On the other hand, as Blau and Meyer abundantly make clear, formal organization oftentimes carries with it structural stasis and inflexibility, the incapacities of expertise and formal authority, ritualism and the perversion of goals, impersonality and alienation, automatism and the constraint of dissent. These unwanted effects of bureaucratization, as noted above, are a leading theme in the critique of modern society by the radical left, whose spokesmen frequently "are more reminiscent of Rousseau than of Marx, with their fierce condemnation of rational organization, their idealization of warm personal relations . . . , and their yearning for a more natural and primitive style of life." But these spokesmen, as Blau and Meyer emphasize, ignore bureaucracy's "essential contribu-tions to many democratic objectives in complex contemporary societies." Clearly, an enormously important lesson for all serious students of social life, and perhaps especially for the "new radicals" and the advocates of a "counter-culture," is the two-faced nature of man's "greatest social invention"; its powerful threat to freedom, spontaneity, and social progress, to be sure; but also its many benefits, both attained and potential, to individual and society. *Bureaucracy in Modern Society* teaches this lesson well.

Amherst, Massachusetts CHARLES H. PAGE
February 1971

Contents

Bureaucracy
in Modern Society

1

Why Study Bureaucracy?

"That stupid bureaucrat!" Who has not felt this way at one time or another? When we are sent from one official to the next without getting the information we want; when lengthy forms we had to fill out in sextuplicate are returned to us because we forgot to cross a "t" or dot an "i"; when our applications are refused on some technicality—those are the times we think of bureaucracy. Colloquially, the term "bureaucracy" has become an epithet which refers to inefficiency and red tape in the government; but this was not its original meaning, and it is not the way the term will be used in this book.

If you alone had the job of collecting the dues in a small fraternity, you could proceed at your own discretion. However, if five persons had this job in a large club, they would find it necessary to organize their work lest some members were asked for dues repeatedly and others never. If hundreds of persons have the assignment of collecting taxes from millions of citizens, their work must be very systematically organized; otherwise chaos would reign and the assignment could not be fulfilled. The type of organization designed to accomplish large-scale administrative tasks by systematically coordinating the work of many individuals is called a bureaucracy. This concept, then, applies to organizing principles that are intended to improve administrative efficiency and that generally do so, although bureaucratization quite often has the opposite effect of producing inefficiency. Since complex administrative problems confront most large organizations, bureaucracy is not confined to the military and civilian branches of the government but is also found in business, unions, churches, universities, and even in baseball clubs.

Interestingly enough, while the term "bureaucratic" is often used as a synonym for inefficiency, at other times it is used to imply ruthless efficiency. Some of the radical criticism of contemporary society, particularly by the New Left, tends to blame bureaucratic institutions for all the evils in today's world—the domination of weak nations by imperialist powers, the oppression of poor people and minority groups, the alienation of youth. There is an element of truth in this criticism, for the bureaucratic form of organization is an effective instrument that helps powerful groups to dominate others, thereby engendering alienation and endangering democracy. However, the criticism is misleading, inasmuch as it attributes the undesirable consequences of fundamental inequalities in economic and political power to the instrument through which this power is exercised. Karl Marx himself, though he condemns bureaucracy in several passages, clearly considers the power differences in the class structure, not bureaucracy, responsible for oppression, exploitation, and alienation.

Bureaucracies are powerful institutions which greatly enhance potential capacities for good or for evil, because they are neutral instruments of rational administration on a large scale. They may facilitate imperialistic expansion and economic exploitation, to the detriment of weak nations and poor people. But these mechanisms of large-scale administration are also required in complex modern societies to achieve democratic objectives, be they raising the standard of living of people, distributing incomes more equitably, or increasing the influence of citizens over their government. To abolish bureaucracy would mean giving up all hope of realizing these objectives. The problem faced by a democratic society is how to gain and maintain democratic control over its bureaucracies so that they will work in the interest of the commonweal. We shall discuss this problem later in this chapter as well as in the last chapter.

The Rationalization of Modern Life

Much of the magic and mystery that used to pervade human life and lend it enchantment has disappeared from the modern world.[1] This is largely the price of rationalization. In olden times, nature was full of mysteries, and man's most serious intellectual endeavors were directed toward discovering the ultimate meaning of his existence. Today, nature holds fewer secrets for us. Scientific advances, however, have not only made it possible to explain many natural phenomena but have also channeled human thinking. Modern man is less concerned than, say, medieval man was with ultimate values and symbolic meanings, with those aspects of mental life that are not subject to scientific inquiry, such as religious truth and artistic creation. This is an age of great scientists and engineers, not of great philosophers or prophets.

The secularization of the world that spells its disenchantment is indicated by the large amount of time we spend in making a living and getting ahead, and the little time we

---

[1] The disenchantment of the world is a main theme running through the writings of the German sociologist Max Weber, whose classical analysis of bureaucratic structure will be discussed presently.

spend in contemplation and religious activities. Compare the low prestige of moneylenders and the high prestige of priests in former eras with the very different positions of bankers and preachers today. Preoccupied with perfecting efficient means for achieving objectives, we tend to forget why we want to reach those goals. Since we neglect to clarify the basic values that determine why some objectives are preferable to others, objectives lose their significance, and their pursuit becomes an end in itself. This tendency is portrayed in Budd Shulberg's novel *What Makes Sammy Run?* The answer to the question in the title is that only running makes him run, because he is so busy trying to get ahead that he has no time to find out where he is going. Continuous striving for success is not Sammy's means for the attainment of certain ends but the very goal of his life.

These consequences of rationalization have often been deplored, and some observers have even suggested that it is not worth the price.[2] There is no conclusive evidence, however, that alienation from profound values is the inevitable and permanent by-product of rationalization, and not merely an expression of its growing pains. The beneficial results of rationalization—notably the higher standard of living and the greater amount of leisure it makes possible, and the raising of the level of popular education it makes necessary—permit an increasing proportion of the population, not just a privileged elite, to participate actively in the cultural life of the society.

Our high standard of living is usually attributed to the spectacular technological developments that have occurred since the Industrial Revolution, but this explanation ignores two related facts. First, the living conditions of most people

[2] See Pitirim Sorokin, *Social and Cultural Dynamics* (New York: American Book, 1937–1941). The author traces fluctuations in cultural emphasis on science and rationality, on the one hand, and faith and supernatural phenomena, on the other, from the earliest times to the present, and vigorously condemns the present trend toward rationalization.

during the early stages of industrialization, after they had moved from the land into the cities with their sweatshops, were probably much worse than they had been before. Dickens depicts these terrible conditions in certain novels, and Marx describes them in his biting critique of the capitalistic economy.[3] Second, major improvements in the standard of living did not take place until administrative procedures as well as the material technology had been revolutionized. Modern machines could not be utilized without the complex administrative machinery needed for running factories employing thousands of workers. It was not so much the invention of new machines as the introduction of mass-production methods that enabled Henry Ford to increase wages and yet produce a car so cheaply that it ceased to be a luxury. When Ford later refused to make further administrative innovations, in the manner of his competitors, his company's position suffered, but after his grandson instituted such changes the company manifested new competitive strength. Rationalization in administration is a prerequisite for the full exploitation of technological knowledge in mass production, and thus for a high standard of living.[4]

Let us examine some of the administrative principles on which the productive efficiency of the modern factory depends. If every worker manufactured a complete car, each would have to be a graduate of an engineering college, and even then he could not do a very good job, since it would be impossible for him to be at once an expert

---

[3] Karl Marx, *Capital* (New York: International Publishers, 1967), Vol. I, Chaps. 26–31.

[4] To be sure, activities of trade unions have greatly contributed to the raising of our standard of living by forcing employers to distribute a larger proportion of their income to workers. Without administrative efficiency in the production and distribution of goods, however, there would be less income to distribute, and fewer goods could be bought with a given amount of income. Moreover, the strength of unions also depends on an efficient administrative machinery.

mechanical engineer, electrical engineer, and industrial designer. Besides, there would not be enough people with engineering degrees in the country to fill all the positions. Specialization permits the employment of many less-trained workers, which lowers production costs. Moreover, whereas the jack-of-all-trades is necessarily master of none, each employee can become a highly skilled expert in his particular field of specialization.

What has been taken apart must be put together again. A high degree of specialization creates a need for a complex system of coordination. No such need exists in the small shop, where the work is less specialized, all workers have direct contact with one another, and the boss can supervise the performance of all of them. The president of a large company cannot possibly discharge his managerial responsibility for coordination through direct consultation with each one of several thousand workers. Managerial responsibility, therefore, is exercised through a hierarchy of authority, which furnishes lines of communication between top management and every employee for obtaining information on operations and transmitting operating directives. (Sometimes, these lines of communication become blocked, and this is a major source of inefficiency in administration.)

Effective coordination requires disciplined performance, which cannot be achieved by supervision alone but must pervade the work process itself. This is the function of rules and regulations that govern operations, whether they specify the dimensions of nuts and bolts or the criteria to be used in promoting subordinates. Even in the ideal case where every employee is a highly intelligent and skilled expert, there is a need for disciplined adherence to regulations. Say one worker had discovered that he could produce bolts of superior quality by making them one-eighth of an inch larger, and another worker had found that he could increase efficiency by making nuts one-eighth of an inch smaller. Although each one made the most rational decision in terms of his own operations, the nuts and bolts would of course be useless because they would not match. How one's own work fits together with that of others is usually far less obvious than in this illustration. For the operations of hundreds of employees to be coordinated, each individual must conform to prescribed standards even in situations where a different course of action appears to him to be most rational. This is a requirement of all teamwork, although in genuine teamwork the rules are not imposed from above but are based on common agreement.

Efficiency also suffers when emotions or personal considerations influence administrative decisions. If the owner of a small grocery expands his business and opens a second store, he may put his son in charge even though another employee is better qualified for the job. He acts on the basis of his personal attachment rather than in the interest of business efficiency. Similarly, an official in a large company might not promote the best-qualified worker to foreman if one of the candidates were his brother. Indeed, his personal feelings could prevent him from recognizing that the qualifications of his brother were inferior. Since the subtle effects of strong emotions cannot easily be suppressed, the best way to check their interference with efficiency is to exclude from the administrative hierarchy those interpersonal relationships that are characterized by emotional attachments. While relatives sometimes work for the same company, typically they are not put in charge of one another. Impersonal relationships assure the detachment necessary if efficiency alone is to govern administrative decisions. However, relationships between employees who have frequent social contacts do not remain purely impersonal, as we shall see.

These four factors—specialization, a hierarchy of authority, a system of rules, and impersonality—are the basic characteristics of bureaucratic organization. Factories are bureaucratically organized, as are government agencies, and if this were not the case they could not operate efficiently on a large scale. Chapter 2 is devoted to a more detailed analysis of bureaucratic structure and the conditions that give rise to bureaucratization. But actual operations do not exactly follow the formal blueprint. To understand how bureaucracies function, we must observe them in action. This is the task of Chapters 3 and 4, which are concerned, respectively, with social processes in bureaucracies and relationships of authority. After discussing the functioning of bureaucracies, we shall turn to the formal structure of bureaucratic organizations in Chapter 5. Chapter 6 explores the question of whether or not bureaucracies can bring about fundamental social change, while Chapter 7 assesses what changes are likely to take place within bureaucracies. In the concluding chapter, we shall examine the consequences of bureaucratization for social change and for democracy. First, however, the question raised in the title of this introductory chapter should be answered: why study bureaucracy?

The Value of Studying Bureaucracy

Learning to understand bureaucracies is more important today than it ever was. It has, moreover, special significance in a democracy. In addition, the study of bureaucratic organization makes a particular contribution to the advancement of sociological knowledge.

Today

Bureaucracy is not a new phenomenon. It existed in simple forms thousands of years ago in Egypt and Rome. But the trend toward bureaucratization has greatly accelerated during the last century. In contemporary society bureaucracy has become a dominant institution, indeed, the institution that epitomizes the modern era. Unless we understand this institutional form, we cannot understand the social life of today.

The enormous size of modern nations and the organizations within them is one reason for the spread of bureaucracy. In earlier periods, most countries were small, even large ones had only a loose central administration, and there were few formal organizations except the government. Modern countries have many millions of citizens, vast armies, giant corporations, huge unions, and numerous large voluntary associations.[5] To be sure, large size is not synonymous with bureaucratic organization. However, the problems posed by administration on a large scale tend to lead to bureaucratization. As a matter of fact, the large organizations that persisted longest in antiquity and even survived this period, the Roman Empire and the Catholic Church, were thoroughly bureaucratized.

In the United States, employment statistics illustrate the trend toward large, bureaucratic organizations. The federal government employed 8,000 civil servants in 1820, a quarter of a million at the beginning of this century, and 3 million in 1970. Still greater is the number of people who work for large-scale private concerns, the extreme example being General Motors with three-quarters of a million employees. Three-quarters of the employees in manufacturing work in establishments with 100 or more employees, and even in the retail trades, the bulwark of small business, more than one-fifth of all employees work in establishments that large.

A large and increasing proportion of the American people spend their working lives as small cogs in complex organizations. And this is not all, for bureaucracies also affect much of the rest of our lives. The employment agency we approach to get a job, and the union we join to protect it; the supermarket and the chain store where we shop, and the hospitals treating our illnesses; the school our children attend, and the political parties for whose candidates we vote; the fraternal organization where we play, and the

[5] See Kenneth Boulding, *The Organizational Revolution* (New York: Harper & Brothers, 1953).

church where we worship—all these more often than not are large organizations of the kind that tends to be bureaucratically organized.

In a Democracy

Bureaucracy, as the foremost theoretician on the subject points out, "is a power instrument of the first order—for the one who controls the bureaucratic apparatus."[6]

> Under normal conditions, the power position of a fully developed bureaucracy is always overtowering. The "political master" finds himself in the position of the "dilettante" who stands opposite the "expert," facing the trained official who stands within the management of administration. This holds whether the "master" whom the bureaucracy serves is a "people," equipped with the weapons of "legislative initiative," the "referendum," and the right to remove officials, or a parliament, elected on a . . . "democratic" basis and equipped with the right to vote a lack of confidence, or with the actual authority to vote it.[7]

Totalitarianism is the polar case of such bureaucratic concentration of power that destroys democratic processes, but not the only one. The same tendency can be observed in political machines that transfer the power that legally belongs to voters to political bosses, in business corporations that vest the power that rightfully belongs to stockholders in corporation officials, and in those unions that bestow the power that rightfully belongs to rank-and-file members upon union leaders. These cases lead some writers to contend that the present trend toward bureaucratization spells the doom of democratic institutions. This may well be too pessimistic a viewpoint, but there can be no doubt that this trend constitutes a challenge. To protect ourselves against this threat, while continuing to utilize these efficient administrative mechanisms, we must first learn fully to under-

[6] H. H. Gerth and C. Wright Mills (eds.), *From Max Weber: Essays in Sociology* (New York: Oxford University Press, 1946), p. 228.
[7] *Ibid.*, p. 232.

stand how bureaucracies function. Knowledge alone is not power, but ignorance surely facilitates subjugation. This is the reason why the study of bureaucratic organization has such great significance in a democracy.

The problem of efficiency versus democracy, which will occupy us at length later, can initially be clarified by distinguishing three types of association. If an association among men is established for the explicit purpose of producing jointly certain end products, whether it be manufacturing cars or winning wars, considerations of efficiency are of primary importance; hence bureaucratization will further the achievement of this objective. However, if an association is established for the purpose of finding intrinsic satisfaction in common activities, say in religious worship, considerations of efficiency are less relevant. When such an association, for instance a religious body, grows so large that administrative problems engender bureaucratization, the pursuit of the original objectives may, indeed, be hampered.[8] Finally, if an association is established for the purpose of deciding upon common goals and courses of action to implement them, which is the function of democratic government (but not that of government agencies), the free expression of opinion must be safeguarded against other considerations, including those of efficiency. Since bureaucratization prevents the attainment of this objective, it must be avoided at all cost. Ideally, organizations of the first type would always be bureaucratized, and those of the last type, never. But one of the difficulties is that many organizations, such as unions, are of a mixed type.

For Sociologists

The study of bureaucratic organization is of special significance for sociologists because it helps them in their task of

[8] For a fuller discussion of this point, see Charles H. Page, "Bureaucracy and the Liberal Church," *Review of Religion*, 17 (1952), 137–150.

finding an order in the complex interdependencies of social phenomena. The sociologist is concerned with explaining patterns of human behavior in terms of relationships among people and characteristics of the organizations, communities, and societies of which they are a part. For example, to explain why some students get poorer grades than others who are no more intelligent, this sociological hypothesis could be advanced: the former have fewer friends and the discomfort of their social isolation interferes with their work. Let us assume we would actually find that the grades of isolated students are lower than those of the rest. Would that prove the hypothesis? By no means, since the difference could be due to the fact that students who appear stupid in class become less popular, or that radicals (or any other group) are discriminated against by teachers and are also disliked by fellow students.

This problem can be solved in the controlled experiment, which makes it possible to demonstrate that a specific factor has certain effects because all other factors are held constant. If two test tubes have exactly the same content and are kept under the same conditions except that one is heated, the changes that occur in one liquid but not in the other must be the result of heat. Many social conditions, however, in contrast to most physical conditions, cannot be duplicated in the laboratory. Although we can make human subjects feel isolated in an experimental session, this is not the same experience as having no friends in college; and other social conditions, such as international warfare, cannot be reproduced in the laboratory at all. This is a dilemma of social research: controlled conditions are required for the testing of hypotheses, but the artificial situation in laboratory experiments is usually not suitable for this purpose. Not that this is an insurmountable difficulty; techniques have been devised to approximate the analytical model of the controlled experiment outside the laboratory. Still, the larger the number of varying factors in the social situation, the smaller is the chance that explanatory hypotheses can be confirmed.

Bureaucracy provides, as it were, a natural laboratory for social research. The formal organization, with its explicit regulations and official positions, constitutes controlled conditions, and these controls have not been artificially introduced by the scientist but are an inherent part of the bureaucratic structure. To be sure, the daily activities and interactions of the members of a bureaucracy cannot be entirely accounted for by the official blueprint. If they could, there would be no need for conducting empirical studies in bureaucracies, since everything about them could be learned by examining organizational charts and procedure manuals. Several factors in addition to official requirements influence daily operations, which means, of course, that conditions are not as fully controlled as in a laboratory experiment. Nevertheless, the explicit formal organization, the characteristics of which can be easily ascertained, reduces the number of variable conditions in the bureaucratic situation and thereby facilitates the search for and the testing of explanatory hypotheses.

There is still another contribution the study of bureaucracy makes to sociology. A central concern of sociologists is the analysis of social structure—whether it is the structure of small groups, organizations, communities, or whole societies. Social structure is an ambiguous term which is given a variety of meanings by different theorists. Thus, some social scientists consider the common values and beliefs that people hold part of the social structure, while others restrict the term to the patterns of relations among individuals, groups, and collectivities (for example, the class structure or the kinship system), and distinguish social structure in this narrower sense from the normative order consisting of common values and beliefs concerning conduct.

Bureaucracies are excellent sites for the study of the relationship between social structure and the normative systems associated with it. A very detailed table of organization describes the bureaucracy's formal structure, and the official charter, rules, and regulations indicate its normative system.

Information about these characteristics of organizations can be readily obtained, and while it does not take into account the informal patterns that emerge (which must be studied separately), it does make possible the study of the relationships among various structural characteristics and between them and official procedures. Such information provides the basis for dealing with important theoretical questions about organizations. One question is whether various aspects of bureaucratization do in fact occur together: For example, is a rigid hierarchy with centralized authority more likely to be found in organizations with detailed bureaucratic rules than in those with less red tape? Another question is how the formal structure of an organization changes as tasks become complex and are largely performed by professional personnel.

Organizations are relatively small compared to communities or whole societies—they have scores or thousands of members, not millions or hundreds of millions. Their boundaries are clear, as most have criteria that define membership. Their purposes or goals are also explicit, which is not the case for families, communities, and societies. Given these characteristics, we can study organizations as total *social systems* by analyzing the relationships among such system properties as size, division of labor, hierarchical structure, formal codes of behavior, and social objectives. This type of analysis not only is of intrinsic interest for clarifying the nature of organizations but also contributes to a general understanding of complex social systems. Hence, the systematic study of the structure of organizations is a first step for developing hypotheses about the theoretical principle that apply to social systems in general.

In summary, the prevalence of bureaucracies in our society furnishes a practical reason for studying them. The fact that they endanger democratic institutions supplies an ideological reason. And the contribution their study can make to sociological knowledge provides a scientific reason for undertaking this task.

2.

Theory
of Bureau

Advancement in any science depends on developments in both theory and empirical research and on a close connection between them. The objectives of science are to improve the accuracy and scope of explanations of phenomena as a basis for better predictability and control. A system of interrelated explanatory propositions is a scientific theory. Not every insight, however, is a scientific proposition; this term refers only to those that have empirical implications that can be confirmed in systematic research, which is not the case for all explanations. Arnold Toynbee's interpretation of history in terms of challenge and response, for instance, although it may provide new insights into the course of history, cannot be empirically tested, since there is no conceivable factual evidence that would clearly disprove it. An important methodological principle of science holds that only those propositions can be empirically corroborated that indicate precisely the evidence necessary for disproving them.

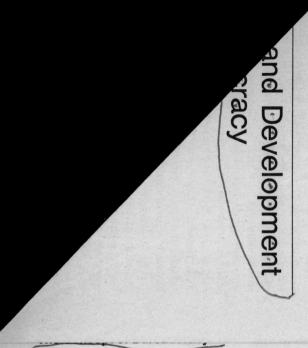

The main characteristics of a bureaucratic structure (in the "ideal-typical" case[1]), according to Weber, are the following:

1. "The regular activities required for the purposes of the organization are distributed in a fixed way as official duties."[2] The clear-cut division of labor makes it possible to employ only specialized experts in each particular position and to make every one of them responsible for the effective performance of his duties. This high degree of specialization has become so much part of our socioeconomic life that we

---

[1] The "ideal type" is discussed later in this chapter.
[2] H. H. Gerth and C. Wright Mills (eds.), *From Max Weber: Essays in Sociology* (New York: Oxford University Press, 1946), p. 196. By permission.

tend to forget that it did not prevail in former eras but is a relatively recent bureaucratic innovation.

2. "The organization of offices follows the principle of hierarchy; that is, each lower office is under the control and supervision of a higher one."[3] Every official in this administrative hierarchy is accountable to his superior for his subordinates' decisions and actions as well as his own. To be able to discharge his responsibility for the work of subordinates, he has authority over them, which means that he has the right to issue directives and they have the duty to obey them. This authority is strictly circumscribed and confined to those directives that are relevant for official operations. The use of status prerogatives to extend the power of control over subordinates beyond these limits does not constitute the legitimate exercise of bureaucratic authority.

3. Operations are governed "by a consistent system of abstract rules . . . [and] consist of the application of these rules to particular cases."[4] This system of standards is designed to assure uniformity in the performance of every task, regardless of the number of persons engaged in it, and the coordination of different tasks. Explicit rules and regulations define the responsibility of each member of the organization and the relationships among them. This does not imply that bureaucratic duties are necessarily simple and routine. It must be remembered that strict adherence to general standards in deciding specific cases characterizes not only the job of the file clerk but also that of the Supreme Court justice. For the former, it may involve merely filing alphabetically; for the latter, it involves interpreting the law of the land in order to settle the most complicated legal issues. Bureaucratic duties range in complexity from one of these extremes to the other.

4. "The ideal official conducts his office . . . [in] a spirit

[3] Max Weber, *The Theory of Social and Economic Organization*, translated by A. M. Henderson and Talcott Parsons (New York: Oxford University Press, 1947), p. 331.
[4] *Ibid.*, p. 330.

of formalistic impersonality, '*Sine ira et studio*,' without hatred or passion, and hence without affection or enthusiasm."[5] For rational standards to govern operations without interference from personal considerations, a detached approach must prevail within the organization and especially toward clients. If an official develops strong feelings about some subordinates or clients, he can hardly help letting those feelings influence his official decisions. As a result, and often without being aware of it himself, he might be particularly lenient in evaluating the work of one of his subordinates or might discriminate against some clients and in favor of others. The exclusion of personal considerations from official business is a prerequisite for impartiality as well as for efficiency. The very factors that make a government bureaucrat unpopular with his clients, an aloof attitude and a lack of genuine concern with them as human beings, actually benefit these clients. Disinterestedness and lack of personal interest go together. The official who does not maintain social distance and becomes personally interested in the cases of his clients tends to be partial in his treatment of them, favoring those he likes over others. Impersonal detachment engenders equitable treatment of all persons and thus equal justice in administration.

5. Employment in the bureaucratic organization is based on technical qualifications and is protected against arbitrary dismissal. "It constitutes a career. There is a system of 'promotions' according to seniority or to achievement, or both."[6] These personnel policies, which are found not only in civil service but also in many private companies, encourage the development of loyalty to the organization and esprit de corps among its members. The consequent identification of employees with the organization motivates them to exert greater efforts in advancing its interests. It may also give rise to a tendency to think of themselves as a

[5] *Ibid.*, p. 340.
[6] *Ibid.*, p. 334.

class apart from and superior to the rest of the society. Among civil servants, this tendency has been more pronounced in Europe, notably in Germany and France, than in the United States, but among military officers, it may be found here too.

6. "Experience tends universally to show that the purely bureaucratic type of administrative organization . . . is, from a purely technical point of view, capable of attaining the highest degree of efficiency."[7] "The fully developed bureaucratic mechanism compares with other organizations exactly as does the machine with non-mechanical modes of production."[8] Bureaucracy solves the distinctive organizational problem of maximizing organizational efficiency, not merely that of individuals.

The superior administrative efficiency of bureaucracy is the expected result of its various characteristics as outlined by Weber. For an individual to work efficiently, he must have the necessary skills and apply them rationally and energetically; but for an organization to operate efficiently, more is required. Every one of its members must have the expert skills needed for the performance of his tasks. This is the purpose of specialization and of employment on the basis of technical qualifications, often ascertained by objective tests. Even experts, however, may be prevented by personal bias from making rational decisions. The emphasis on impersonal detachment is intended to eliminate this source of irrational action. But individual rationality is not enough. As noted above, if the members of the organization were to make rational decisions independently, their work would not be coordinated and the efficiency of the organization would suffer. Hence there is need for discipline to limit the scope of rational discretion, which is met by the system of rules and regulations and the hierarchy of supervision. Moreover, personnel policies that permit employees

[7] *Ibid.*, p. 337.
[8] Gerth and Mills, *op. cit.*, p. 214.

to feel secure in their jobs and to anticipate advancements for faithful performance of duties discourage attempts to impress superiors by introducing clever innovations, which may endanger coordination. Lest this stress on disciplined obedience to rules and rulings undermine the employee's motivation to devote his energies to his job, incentives for exerting effort must be furnished. Personnel policies that cultivate organizational loyalty and that provide for promotion on the basis of merit serve this function. In other words, the combined effect of bureaucracy's characteristics is to create social conditions which constrain each member of the organization to act in ways that, whether they appear rational or otherwise from his individual standpoint, further the rational pursuit of organizational objectives.

Without explicitly stating so, Weber supplies a *functional* analysis of bureaucracy. In this type of analysis, a social structure is explained by showing how each of its elements contributes to its persistence and effective operations. Concern with discovering all these contributions, however, entails the danger that the scientist may neglect to investigate the disturbances that various elements produce in the structure. As a result, his presentation may make the social structure appear to function more smoothly than it actually does, since he neglects the disruptions that do in fact exist. To protect ourselves against this danger, it is essential to extend the analysis beyond the mere consideration of functions, as Robert K. Merton points out.[9] Of particular importance for avoiding false implications of stability and for explaining social change is the study of *dysfunctions*, those consequences that interfere with adjustment and create problems in the structure.[10]

A reexamination of the foregoing discussion of bureau-

---

[9] Robert K. Merton, *Social Theory and Social Structure*, 3rd ed. (New York: Free Press, 1968), pp. 73–138.

[10] For a general discussion of functional analysis, see Ely Chinoy, *Sociological Perspective* (New York: Random House, 1968), Chap. 5.

cratic features in the light of the concept of dysfunction reveals inconsistencies and conflicting tendencies. If reserved detachment characterizes the attitudes of the members of the organization toward one another, it is unlikely that high esprit de corps will develop among them. The strict exercise of authority in the interest of discipline induces subordinates, anxious to be highly thought of by their superiors, to conceal defects in operations from superiors, and this obstruction of the flow of information upward in the hierarchy impedes effective management. Insistence on conformity also tends to engender rigidities in official conduct and to inhibit the rational exercise of judgment needed for the efficient performance of tasks. If promotions are based on merit, many employees will not experience advancements in their careers. If they are based primarily on seniority so as to give employees this experience and thereby to encourage them to become identified with the organization, the promotion system will not furnish strong incentives for exerting efforts and excellent performance. These illustrations suffice to indicate that the same factor that enhances efficiency in one respect often threatens it in another; it may have *both* functional and dysfunctional consequences.

Weber was well aware of such contradictory tendencies in the bureaucratic structure. But since he treats dysfunctions only incidentally, his discussion leaves the impression that administrative efficiency in bureaucracies is more stable and less problematical than it actually is. In part, it was his intention to present an idealized image of bureaucratic structure, and he used the conceptual tool appropriate for this purpose. Let us critically examine this conceptual tool.

Implications of the Ideal-Type Construct

Weber dealt with bureaucracy as what he termed an "ideal type." This methodological concept does not represent an average of the attributes of all existing bureaucracies (or other social structures), but a pure type, derived by abstracting the most characteristic bureaucratic aspects of all known organizations. Since perfect bureaucratization is never fully realized, no empirical organization corresponds exactly to this scientific construct.

The criticism has been made that Weber's analysis of an imaginary ideal type does not provide understanding of concrete bureaucratic structures. But this criticism obscures the fact that the ideal-type construct is intended as a guide in empirical research, not as a substitute for it. By indicating the characteristics of bureaucracy in its pure form, it directs the researcher to those aspects of organizations that he must examine in order to determine the extent of their bureaucratization. This is the function of all conceptual schemes: to specify the factors that must be taken into consideration in investigations and to define them clearly.

The ideal typical model of bureaucracy, however, is not simply a conceptual scheme. It includes not only definitions of concepts but also implicit generalizations about the relationships among them, and specifically the hypothesis that the diverse bureaucratic characteristics increase administrative efficiency. If certain attributes (for example, specialization, hierarchy, rules, and impersonality) are distinctive of bureaucracy compared to other forms of administration, and if bureaucracy is the most efficient form of administration, then at least some of the attributes of bureaucracy must be conducive to efficient operations. Whereas conceptual definitions are presupposed in research and not subject to verification by research findings, hypotheses concerning relationships among factors are subject to such verification. Whether strict hierarchical authority, for example, indeed furthers efficiency is a question of empirical fact and not one of definition. But as the scientific construct Weber intended it to be, the ideal type cannot be refuted by empirical evidence. If a study of several organizations were to find that strict hierarchical authority is not related to efficiency, this would not prove that no such relationship exists in the ideal-type bureaucracy; it would show only that these organizations are not fully bureaucratized. Since generalizations about idealized states defy testing in systematic research, they have no place in science. On the other hand, if empirical evidence is taken into consideration and generalizations are modified accordingly, we deal with prevailing tendencies in bureaucratic structures and no longer with a pure type.

Two misleading implications of the ideal-type conception of bureaucracy deserve special mention. The student of social organization is concerned with the patterns of activities and interactions that reveal how social conduct is organized, and not with exceptional deviations from these patterns. The fact that one official becomes excited and shouts at his colleague, or that another arrives late at the office, is unimportant in understanding the organization, except that the rare occurrence of such events indicates that they are idiosyncratic, differing from the prevailing patterns. Weber's decision to treat only the purely formal organization of bureaucracy implies that all deviations from these formal requirements are idiosyncratic and of no interest for the student of organization. Later empirical studies have shown this approach to be misleading. Informal relations and unofficial practices develop among the members of bureaucracies and assume an organized form without being officially sanctioned. Chester I. Barnard, one of the first to call attention to this phenomenon, held that these "informal organizations are necessary to the operations of formal organizations."[11] These informal patterns, in contrast to exceptional occurrences, as we shall see in Chapter 3, are a regular part of bureaucratic organizations and therefore must be taken into account in their analysis.

Weber's approach also implies that any deviation from

[11] Chester I. Barnard, *The Functions of the Executive* (Cambridge: Harvard University Press, 1948), p. 123.

the formal structure is detrimental to administrative efficiency. Since the ideal type is conceived as the perfectly efficient organization, all differences from it must necessarily interfere with efficiency. There is considerable evidence that suggests the opposite conclusion; informal relations and unofficial practices often contribute to efficient operations. In any case, the significance of these unofficial patterns for operations cannot be determined in advance on theoretical grounds but only on the basis of empirical investigations. Before examining such case studies of bureaucracies we shall explore the conditions that give rise to bureaucratization.

Conditions that Give Rise to Bureaucratization

To say that there is a historical trend toward bureaucracy is to state that many organizations change from less to more bureaucratic forms of administration. Yet the historical trend itself and the changes in any specific organization are different phenomena. Both are expressions of the process of bureaucratization, but since different conditions account for them, they will be discussed separately.

Historical Conditions

One of the historical conditions that favors the development of bureaucracy is a money economy. This is not an absolute prerequisite. Bureaucracies based on compensation in kind existed, for example, in Egypt, Rome, and China. Generally, however, a money economy permits the payment of regular salaries, which, in turn, creates the combination of dependence and independence that is most conducive to the faithful performance of bureaucratic duties. Unpaid volunteers are too independent of the organization to submit unfailingly to its discipline. Slaves, on the other hand, are too dependent on their masters to have the incentive to assume responsibilities and carry them out on their own initiative. The economic dependence of the salaried employee on his job and his freedom to advance himself in his career engender the orientation toward work required for disciplined *and* responsible conduct. Consequently, there were few bureaucracies prior to the development of a monetary system and the abolition of slavery.

It has already been mentioned that sheer size encourages the development of bureaucracies, since they are mechanisms for executing large-scale administrative tasks. The large modern nation, business, or union is more likely to be bureaucratized than was its smaller counterpart in the past. More important than size as such, however, is the emergence of special administrative problems. Thus in ancient Egypt the complex job of constructing and regulating waterways throughout the country gave rise to the first known large-scale bureaucracy in history. In other countries, notably those with long frontiers requiring defense, bureaucratic methods were introduced to solve the problem of organizing an effective army and the related one of raising taxes for this purpose. England, without land frontiers, maintained only a small army in earlier centuries, which may in part account for the fact that the trend toward bureaucratization was less pronounced there than in continental nations, which had to support large armies. Weber cites the victory of the Puritans under the leadership of Cromwell over the Cavaliers, who fought more heroically but with less discipline, as an illustration of the superior effectiveness of a bureaucratized army.[12]

The capitalistic system also has furthered the advance of bureaucracy. The rational estimation of economic risks,

[12] Gerth and Mills, *op. cit.*, pp. 256–257. The advanced student will have recognized the indebtedness of the foregoing discussion to Weber's (pp. 204–216). It goes without saying that Weber's fund of historical knowledge and his profound theoretical insights about bureaucracy can be acknowledged as outstanding contributions in the field, even if one rejects his use of the ideal-type construct.

which is presupposed in capitalism, requires that the regular processes of the competitive market not be interrupted by external forces in unpredictable ways. Arbitrary actions of political tyrants interfere with the rational calculation of gain or loss, and so do banditry, piracy, and social upheavals. The interest of capitalism demands, therefore, not only the overthrow of tyrannical rulers but also the establishment of governments strong enough to maintain order and stability. Note that after the American Revolution such representatives of the capitalists as Alexander Hamilton advocated a strong federal government, while representatives of farmers, in the manner of Jefferson, favored a weak central government.

Capitalism then promotes effective and extensive operations of the government. It also leads to bureaucratization in other spheres. The expansion of business firms and the consequent removal of most employees from activities directly governed by the profit principle make it increasingly necessary to introduce bureaucratic methods of administration for the sake of efficiency. These giant corporations, in turn, constrain workers, who no longer can bargain individually with an employer they know personally, to organize into large unions with complex administrative machineries. Strange as it may seem, the free-enterprise system fosters the development of bureaucracy in the government, in private companies, and in unions.

These historical conditions were not causes of bureaucracy in the usual sense of the term. Evidently, a large and effective army did not cause bureaucracy; on the contrary, bureaucratic methods of operation produced an effective large army. The need for these methods, however, arose in the course of trying to build such an army without them and helped bring about a bureaucratic form of organization. The qualifying word "helped" is essential. If needs inevitably created ways of meeting them, human society would be paradise. In this world, wishes are not horses, and beggars do not ride. Social needs, just as individual ones, often persist without being met. Knowledge of the conditions that engendered a need for bureaucracy does not answer the question: what made its development actually possible under some circumstances and not under others? The Cavaliers were in need of a better fighting force, as their defeat demonstrates. Why was it not they but the Puritans who organized a disciplined army?

In *The Protestant Ethic and the Spirit of Capitalism*, Weber indirectly answers this question. He shows that the Reformation—especially Calvinism, the religious doctrine of the Puritans—apart from its spiritual significance, had the social consequence of giving rise to this-worldly asceticism, a disciplined devotion to hard work in the pursuit of one's vocation. The Protestant has no Pope or priest to furnish spiritual guidance and absolve him for his sins, but must ultimately rely on his own conscience and faith; this encourages the emergence of self-imposed discipline. The strong condemnation of pleasure and emotions, exemplified by the Puritan "blue laws," generates the sobriety and detachment conducive to rational conduct. Moreover, in contrast to Catholicism and even Lutheranism, Calvinism does not emphasize that the existing order is God's creation but that it has been corrupted by man's sinfulness. Man's religious duty is not to adapt to this wicked world, nor to withdraw from it into a monastery, but to help transform it *in majorem gloriam Dei* through methodical efforts in his everyday life and regular work. The anxieties aroused by the doctrine of double predestination, according to which man cannot affect his predestined fate or even know whether he will be saved or damned, reinforced the Calvinist's tendency to adopt a rigorous discipline and immerse himself in his work as a way of relieving his anxieties.

Protestantism, therefore, has transplanted the ascetic devotion to disciplined hard work (which must be distinguished from the exertion of effort as a means for reaching specific ends) from monastic life, to which it was largely confined earlier, to the mundane affairs of economic life.

Although the explicit purposes of the Reformation were other-worldly and not this-worldly, the psychological orientation it created had the unanticipated consequence of helping to revolutionize the secular world. For without this orientation toward ceaseless effort and rational conduct as intrinsic moral values, Weber argues convincingly, modern capitalism could not have emerged when it did, and neither, it should be added, could full-blown bureaucracy have developed, because it too depends on rational discipline.[13]

Structural Conditions

The historical conditions that led to the pervasiveness of bureaucracy today do not, of course, explain why some organizations in contemporary society are highly bureaucratized and others are not. These variations raise the problem of the conditions within a given social structure that give rise to its bureaucratization. A recent empirical study is concerned with this problem.

Alvin W. Gouldner investigated the process of bureaucratization in a gypsum plant.[14] After the death of the old manager, the company that owned the plant appointed a man who had been in charge of one of its smaller factories as his successor. The new manager, anxious to prove himself worthy of the promotion by improving productivity, was faced with special difficulties. He was not familiar with the ways of working that had become customary in this plant, had not established informal relations with his subordinates, and did not command the allegiance of workers, who still felt loyal to his predecessor. To marshal the willing support of workers and induce them to identify with his managerial objectives, he attempted to cultivate informal relations with

---

[13] For a fuller discussion of the unintended effects of Protestantism, see Elizabeth K. Nottingham, *Religion: A Sociological Review* (New York: Random House, 1971).

[14] Alvin W. Gouldner, *Patterns of Industrial Bureaucracy* (Glencoe, Ill.: Free Press, 1954).

them; but this could not be done overnight. In the meantime, he found it necessary to discharge his managerial
responsibilities by resorting to formal procedures. In the
absence of informal channels of communication to keep him
informed about the work situation, the new manager instituted a system of regular operational reports for this purpose. Since he did not know the workers well enough to
trust them, he closely checked on their operations and
ordered his lieutenants to establish strict discipline. When
some of these lieutenants, used to the more lenient ways of
the former manager, failed to adopt rigorous methods of
close supervision, he replaced them by outsiders who were
more sympathetic with his disciplinarian approach. These
innovations alienated workers and deepened the gulf between them and the manager, with the result that he had to
rely increasingly on formal bureaucratic methods of administration.

> The role of the successor . . . confronted Peele with distinc-
> tive problems. He had to solve these problems if he wished to
> hold his job as manager. In the process of solving them, the
> successor was compelled to use bureaucratic methods. Peele
> intensified bureaucracy not merely because he wanted to, not
> necessarily because he liked bureaucracy, nor because he
> valued it above other techniques, but also because he was
> constrained to do so by the tensions of his succession.[15]

In the interest of his objective of gaining control over the
operations in the plant, it was necessary for the successor to
introduce bureaucratic procedures. At the same time, for
workers to realize their objective of maintaining some independent control over their own work, it was necessary for
them to oppose the introduction of disciplinarian measures.
As noted above, the existence of a need does not explain
why it is met. In this case, two conflicting needs existed side
by side, with the "victor" determined by the power structure in the organization. The powerful position of the

[15] *Ibid.*, pp. 97–98.

manager was responsible for his ability to meet his need by bureaucratizing operations, as indicated by the following comparison with a situation where he was not similarly successful.

This plant consisted of a gypsum mine and a wallboard factory, but the process of bureaucratic formalization was largely confined to the factory. Stronger informal ties and more pronounced group solidarity prevailed among miners than among factory workers, partly as a consequence of the common danger to which they were exposed in the mine. Miners were highly motivated to work hard, and they had developed their own unofficial system of assigning tasks among themselves; for instance, new miners had to do the dirty jobs. Hence there was less need in the mine for formal discipline and rules prescribing exact duties. Nevertheless, Peele attempted to formalize operating procedures there, too. The strength of their informal organization, however, made it possible for miners, in contrast to factory workers, effectively to resist these attempts. The process of bureaucratic formalization generated by succession in management is not inevitable; collective resistance can arrest it.

The miners, so to speak, had evolved an unofficial bureaucratic apparatus of their own. Their effective informal organization, by regulating their work, took the place of a more formal system of control and simultaneously gave them sufficient power to defeat endeavors to impose a formal system of discipline upon them against their will. Did efficiency suffer? Gouldner implies it did not, although he does not specifically deal with this question. In any case, the conduct of the miners calls attention, once more, to the importance of informal relations and unofficial practices in bureaucratic structures.

Time of Origin

The historical period in which organizations were established affects their characteristics. Armies, which originated many centuries ago, still have today a more authoritarian structure than factories, which are of more recent origin. For bureaucratic structures are characterized by a great deal of inertia, and they often resist innovations, even those that would improve efficiency. When an organization is founded, its structure usually reflects the latest in both technology and administrative practices. Once it has been founded, however, its structure tends to remain intact for some time, little affected by new technologies and often insensitive to changes in operating procedures that would enable it to perform better.

A study by Arthur Stinchcombe classified major industries according to their age and certain characteristics of the work force which were reported in the 1950 census.[16] The analysis focused on four variables: the proportion of unpaid family workers in an industry, the proportion of managerial posts occupied by the owner's family, the number of clerical employees, and the proportion of administrators with professional qualifications. The oldest industries—agriculture, wholesale and retail trades, water transportation, and the like—had in 1950 relatively many unpaid family employees and family members acting as managers, whereas the numbers of clerks and of professionals were relatively low. Industries formed later, in the early nineteenth century, by contrast, had nearly no unpaid family members in 1950 (though relatives remained as managers), and the clerical component was substantial—about half of administrative employees were clerks. The woodworking, apparel, textile, and banking industries were included in this group. Late nineteenth-century organizations—railroads, mining, and metals firms—clearly separated ownership from managerial responsibility; that is, the proportion of family members acting as managers was very small. Again, the clerical component was quite large in these industries. Finally, industries established in this century are similar to

[16] Arthur Stinchcombe, "Social Structure and Organizations," in James March (ed.), *Handbook of Organizations* (Chicago: Rand McNally, 1965), pp. 155–160.

their nineteenth-century counterparts except that they employ many professionals. With only one exception (automobile repairs), industries in this category require professional qualifications of more than half of their managers.

Stinchcombe's data would seem to lend credence to the notion that bureaucracies develop in stages. First, cash salaries replace unpaid work by family members. Then, a clerical component is added, and owners are separated from management. Finally, managers are expected to have professional qualifications. The data suggest that newer industries are most bureaucratized, in the sense of having large administrative machineries and of selecting managers on the basis of impersonal rational criteria. Many organizations founded in the nineteenth century have not altered their original structures, perhaps because they have no need to do so, but more likely because they have resisted change. One has only to consult the business pages to find that older industries are generally less profitable than newer ones, which suggests that their efficiency has suffered from lack of innovation. We must conclude, therefore, that the conditions conducive to rationalization or bureaucratization do not necessarily give rise to it in already established organizations.

Resistance to change in organizations has many sources. Change often endangers careers and disturbs vested interest, generating resistance against it. It seems to require a crisis or a change of management to precipitate reorganization, at least in large industries. The historian Alfred Chandler shows in case studies of four corporations—DuPont, General Motors, Sears Roebuck, and Standard Oil of New Jersey—that this is the situation. All four suffered considerable declines in business before they considered reorganization and adopted a modern decentralized structure.[17] Finally, an unpublished study by Jacques Gellard shows

---

[17] Alfred Chandler, *Strategy and Structure* (Cambridge: MIT Press, 1962).

that recently appointed managers are considerably more likely than old-timers to institute change in American government finance departments.[18] To overcome bureaucratic inertia seems to require new organizations or new managers, unencumbered by traditions and personal loyalties, and not already enmeshed in the social processes that characterize the interpersonal relations in the organization. We now turn to an examination of these social processes.

[18] Jacques Gellard, "Determinants and Consequences of Executive Succession in Government Finance Agencies" (unpublished M.A. thesis, University of Chicago, 1967).

3

Bureaucracy
in Process

A bureaucracy in operation appears quite different from the abstract portrayal of its formal structure. Many official rules are honored in the breach; the members of the organization act as human beings—often friendly and sometimes disgruntled—rather than like dehumanized impersonal machines.

But this contradiction between official requirements and actual conduct in bureaucracies may be more apparent than real. Perhaps the violation of some rules is inconsequential for the organization, and the essential regulations are regularly obeyed. It is also possible that a detached attitude is required only in those relationships that are involved in the transaction of official business, such as employee-client or subordinate-superior, and congenial informality is confined to relationships between employees who work next to one another but not with one another, such as the members of a stenographic pool. However, even if such clear-cut divisions between formal and informal spheres were always to exist, which is questionable, it would still be relevant to inquire whether informal relations and unofficial practices have any significant effects on operations and the achievement of organizational objectives. This is the task of the present chapter.

Bureaucracy's Other Face

Cases from four different kinds of organization have been selected for presentation. They deal, respectively, with a military, an industrial, a civil service, and a police organization. All of them reveal "bureaucracy's other face," as Charles H. Page calls the unofficial activities and interactions that are so prominent in the daily operations of formal organizations. These concrete cases furnish the basis for a reexamination of the concept of bureaucratic organization and its relation to administrative efficiency.

IN THE NAVY

The existence and importance of the informal structure of the Navy would hardly be denied by any experienced participant . . . Like the formal, it consists of rules, groupings, and sanctioned systems of procedure. They are informal because they are never recorded in the codes or official blueprints and because they are generated and maintained with a degree of spontaneity always lacking in the activities which make up the formal structure. These rules, groupings, and procedures do, nevertheless, form a structure, for, though not *officially* recognized, they are clearly and semipermanently established, they are just as "real" and just as compelling on the membership as the elements of the official structure, and they maintain their existence and social significance throughout many changes of personnel. . . .

[The newcomer] has two large segments of Navy organization to learn. The high-pressure instruction of the indoctrination school or boot camp, the Navy teacher and his own study of the documents can reveal the intricacies of the

Navy's formal structure. . . . But knowledge of the informal structure, which is at least as necessary for successful participation, must be gained through experience in the group itself. . . .

Many pressing problems develop within the Navy, *efficient* solutions for which are not possible within the framework of the official institutional structure. . . . Such a problem is the constant and, to the initiated, conspicuous one of official communication between officers. Official communications in most cases must, according to regulations, be routed through the "chain of command" for whatever endorsements the officers in the chain judge appropriate. . . . Yet very frequently the circumvention of this regulation appears as precisely the solution of a pressing problem. When such a development occurs the individuals involved, if they are sophisticated in the ways of their organization, will operate on the level of the informal structure wherein a solution is usually possible, and will thereby avoid that bureaucratic frustration so frequently felt by those who are strict followers of "the book." . . .

One extreme example, an island air base whose position and absence of native population guaranteed almost no contact with extra-Navy persons, had experienced a major structural change from the time it had been based in the United States. In this case the informal structure had almost altogether lost its private sanctification and stood, in large measure, as the officially recognized pattern of this group of temporary island residents. One visiting officer described this as a "breakdown" of the organization. This was clearly not the case, as shown by the high morale and the effective accomplishment of missions. What had "broken down" was a large part of the formal structure, or rather it had been submerged as the informal structure rose into overt recognition and use. Fortunately the "skipper" as well as several other officers and petty officers were "natural leaders": their status and role definitions were somewhat parallel in the two structures. However, unmistakable indications of the superordination of the informal included the replacement of the social isolation of the commanding officer by his very keen participation in all activities of the unit, the submergence of the rejected types whatever their rank or rate to the informally defined roles,

the emergence of the natural leaders to what amounted to
official recognition, the abandonment of most of the officially
governing protocol (except in the treatment of visitors), and
accomplishment of the day-to-day and long-run tasks with
efficiency, zeal, and spontaneous initiative not characteristic of
official bureaucratic machinery.[1]

IN A FACTORY

Of the fourteen men, or operators, as they were called in
the Western Electric Company, who were regularly in the
Observation Room, nine were wiremen, . . . three were
soldermen, . . . and two were inspectors. . . . The men were
engaged in making parts of switches for central office telephone equipment. Specifically, they were connecting wires to
banks of terminals. . . . A wireman took the necessary number of banks for an equipment and placed them in a holder or
fixture on a workbench. Then he connected the terminals of
the banks together in a certain order with wire. . . . A wireman worked on two equipments at a time. Having finished a
level on one equipment, he moved to the second equipment. In
the meantime, a solderman fixed in place the finished connections of the first equipment, and an inspector tested and
scrutinized the work of both men. . . .

Let us now turn to some of the activities, over and above
each man's special job, that were observed in the room. One
of the commonest was helping another man out by doing
some of his wiring for him when he had fallen behind. Although no formal rule of the company said that one man
should not help another, helping was in practice forbidden, on
the theory that the jobs were one-man jobs and that each man
could do his own best. Nevertheless a good deal of help was
given. The wiremen said it made them feel good to be helped.
. . . Everyone took part in helping. Unlike some other activities, it was not confined to one social group. . . .

In the lunch hour and from time to time during the work,
the men in the room took part in all sorts of games. Almost
anything was an excuse for a bet: matching coins, lagging

[1] Charles H. Page, "Bureaucracy's Other Face," *Social Forces*, 25
(1946), 89–91. By permission.

coins, shooting craps, cards, combinations of digits in the
serial numbers of weekly pay checks. Pools were organized on
horse racing, baseball, and quality records. . . . Participation
in games occurred for the most part within two groups . . . ,
a group at the front of the room . . . [and] a group at the
back. . . . The material collected by the observer could also
be interpreted to show that friendships or antagonisms existed
between certain men in the room. . . . Except for a friendship between [two men], all friendships occurred within one
or the other of the two groups already mapped out on the
basis of participation in games. . . .

Roethlisberger and Dickson sum up all this evidence by
saying that, although the members of the Bank Wiring Observation Room were pulled together in some ways, for instance,
in mutual help and in restriction of output, in others they
were divided. In particular, there were two cliques in the
room, whose membership was approximately that revealed by
participation in games. . . . [But three men] were in no sense
members of either clique, [two of them] attracting much
antagonism. Each clique had its own games and activities,
noticeably different from those of the other group. . . .

If, as we have seen, the output rates of the wiremen could
not be correlated with their intelligence or dexterity, they
could clearly be correlated with clique membership. . . .
[The members of one clique] had the lowest output.[2] *of two*

IN A GOVERNMENT AGENCY

The principal duties of agents were carried out in the field.
Cases of firms to be investigated were assigned to them individually by the supervisor. Processing a case involved an audit
of the books and records of the firm, interviews with the
employer (or his representative) and a sample of employees,
the determination of the existence of legal violation and the

[2] Condensed from *The Human Group* by George C. Homans, copyright 1950, by Harcourt, Brace and Company, Inc., pp. 54–55, 66,
68–72. The empirical study of the Bank Wiring Observation Room,
which Homans summarizes in this book, and in which he par-
ticipated, is fully reported in F. J. Roethlisberger and William J.
Dickson, *Management and the Worker* (Cambridge: Harvard University Press, 1946), pp. 379–548.

appropriate action to be taken, and negotiations with employers. . . . If an agent encountered a problem he could not solve, he was expected to consult his supervisor, who, if he could not furnish the requested advice himself, gave the agent permission to consult a staff attorney. Agents were not allowed to consult anyone else directly, not even their colleagues. . . .

Agents, however, were reluctant to reveal to their supervisor their inability to solve a problem for fear that their ratings would be adversely affected. . . . Their need for getting advice without exposing their difficulties to the supervisor constrained agents to consult one another, in violation of the official rule. . . .

A consultation can be considered an exchange of values; both participants gain something, and both have to pay a price. The questioning agent is enabled to perform better than he could otherwise have done, without exposing his difficulties to the supervisor. By asking for advice, he implicitly pays his respect to the superior proficiency of his colleague. This acknowledgment of inferiority is the cost of receiving assistance. The consultant gains prestige, in return for which he is willing to devote some time to the consultation and permit it to disrupt his own work. The following remark of an agent illustrates this: "I like giving advice. It's flattering, I suppose, if you feel that the others come to you for advice."

The expert whose advice was often sought by colleagues obtained social evidence of his superior abilities. This increased his confidence in his own decisions, and thus improved his performance as an investigator. . . . The role of the agent who frequently solicited advice was less enviable, even though he benefited most directly from this unofficial practice. Asking a colleague for guidance was less threatening than asking the supervisor, but the repeated admission of his inability to solve his own problems also undermined the self-confidence of an agent and his standing in the group. The cost of advice became prohibitive if the consultant, after the questioner had subordinated himself by asking for help, was in the least discouraging—by postponing a discussion or by revealing his impatience during one. To avoid such rejections, agents usually consulted a colleague with whom they were friendly, even if he was not an expert. . . .

An agent who worked on an interesting case and encountered strange problems often told his fellow agents about it.
. . . These presentations of complex cases assisted the speaker
in solving his problems. They were consultations in disguise.
. . . The agent who attempted to arrive at decisions while
sitting alone at his desk defined the situation as preparing the
case for submission to the supervisor. His anxiety, engendered
by the supervisor's evaluation of his decisions, interfered most
with clear thinking in this situation. Instead of trying to make
important official decisions, an agent could discuss the interesting aspects of his case with one of his colleagues. This situation, defined as a discussion among friends, did not evoke
anxiety. On the contrary, it destroyed the anxiety which per-
vaded the decision-making process.

The listener was not merely a friend but a fellow specialist
in solving the problems which occurred in investigations. This
created the possibility of interruption, if the suggested interpretation required correction. A listener might remind the
speaker that he forgot to take some factor into account, or
that the data lend themselves to alternative conclusions. The
assent implicit in the absence of interruptions and in attentive
listening destroyed the doubts that continuously arose in the
process of making many minor decisions in order to arrive at
a conclusion. The admiration for the clever solution of the
problem advanced, expressed by interested questions and
appreciative comments, increased the speaker's confidence in
his partial solutions while groping for the final one. By reducing his anxiety, "thinking out loud" enabled an official to
associate relevant pieces of information and pertinent regulations, and thus to arrive at decisions of which he might not
have thought while alone. . . .

[This pattern of explicit and disguised consultations] transformed an aggregate of individuals who happened to have the
same supervisor into a cohesive group. The recurrent experience of being dependent on the group, whose members
furnished needed help, and of being appreciated by the others
in the group, as indicated by their solicitations for assistance,
created strong mutual bonds. . . . Second, this practice contributed to operating efficiency, because it improved the
quality of the decisions of agents. Every agent knew that he
could obtain help with solving problems whenever he needed

it. This knowledge, reinforced by the feeling of being an integrated member of a cohesive group, decreased anxiety about making decisions. Simultaneously, being often approached for advice raised the self-confidence of an investigator. The very existence of this practice enhanced the ability of all agents, experts as well as others, to make decisions independently.[3]

IN A POLICE DEPARTMENT

The police in a small town may believe that they are treating equals equally even when they do not treat everybody the same (by, for example, an arrest). With their more intimate knowledge of the community, they can make more discriminating judgments about who is equal to whom.

In Brighton, for example, there was a series of incidents involving a Peeping Tom. The police knew the culprit, a minor executive of an important local firm. When such an incident was reported the police would call the man's wife and tell her, "Your husband's at it again." An arrest, they told the interviewer, would be difficult to make because the victim would often be reluctant to sign a complaint, but a serious effort to secure an arrest, to say nothing of the arrest itself, would make public the behavior of the culprit and no doubt cost him his job. The embarrassment of being reported to his wife was punishment enough. On another occasion the police found the daughter of a prominent local citizen staggering drunk down the street at night with practically no clothes on. They brought her to the station and, although she was very abusive, made no arrest. Instead, the police photographed her in her disorderly condition and showed the picture to her parents to convince them of the seriousness of the problem and to induce them to "do something." The incident was kept out of the town newspaper, which ordinarily prints almost all local police news. At the same time, the officers involved were disgusted to encounter a family that "had everything" but could not handle its own children. "Most of these kids could

---

[3] Peter M. Blau, *The Dynamics of Bureaucracy*, 2nd ed. (Chicago: University of Chicago Press, 1963), pp. 121, 126–128, 130–133, 135. Copyright 1955, 1963 by the University of Chicago. Reprinted by permission of the University of Chicago Press.

be straightened out at home if the parents only took the time to give them a little disciplining," said one officer, "but you don't find that much anymore." Nonetheless, they were sure they had done the right thing, because they had no further trouble with the young lady.

Officers who stop motorists for traffic violations will take into account who is involved, and his attitude, in determining whether a ticket should be issued. One patrolman told an interviewer that if the driver is a doctor or a clergyman, "We just like to warn (them) to slow down for their own good; they may be tired and in a hurry to get home from the hospital."

A traffic ticket once issued in Brighton cannot be fixed—it is a numbered form, all of which must be accounted for to the state. But the police are aware that people who feel unjustly ticketed will try to intervene with the judge or with other town leaders. A senior police officer explained what usually happens: "I can't do anything about a traffic ticket. The judge, he can . . . do anything he wants with it . . . I'm glad. I'd just as soon not get involved in that. I will write a note to the judge asking for leniency in certain cases. I had one involving . . . a big political figure. . . . When it came in I got a phone call saying that, 'Do you know that one of your men just ticketed X's car?' I told him I couldn't do anything about it, but that I would write a letter to the judge explaining what had happened and ask him to go easy. I'm not sure what happened, but I imagine the judge probably dismissed or suspended (the sentence)."

A small department may be more sensitive to circumstances of personality and politics, but by the same token this sensitivity need have nothing to do—indeed, it would create problems if it *did* have something to do—with vulgar bribery. A bribe induces an officer to act other than as his duty requires. Its value requires that an officer have something to sell—freedom from an arrest he is otherwise empowered to make—and that a citizen be willing to buy. Ideally, the transaction should be secret; even if higher police officials were willing to tolerate it, they could rarely do so publicly, and few important citizens concerned about their reputation want to be known in a small town as persons who buy special privileges. But keeping secrets in a small town is not easy. More important, it is not necessary—the officer rarely has anything to sell because his superiors expect him to treat "somebodies" different from "nobodies." A prominent man who is drunk in a public place will, unless he behaves in an extraordinary manner, be taken home or turned over to friends. A shabbily dressed itinerant with no family or friends who commits the same offense will be arrested—there is no place to take him, it is unlikely that embarrassment or a hangover will prove an effective punishment, and he may, lacking a place to stay, hurt himself or endanger others.[4]

Organization of Work Groups

When we examine sufficiently small segments of bureaucracies to observe their operations in detail, we discover patterns of activities and interactions that cannot be accounted for by the official structure. Whether the work group is part of the armed forces, a factory, civil service, or the police, it is characterized by a network of informal relations and a set of unofficial practices which have been called its "informal organization." This concept calls attention to the fact that deviations from the formal blueprint are socially organized patterns and not merely the consequence of fortuitous personality differences. Helping others or playing games was the established practice in the Bank Wiring Observation Room, not a manifestation of the rebellious personality of one or the other individual. Variations in productivity were not due to the fact that the mechanical ability of some workers happened to be superior to that of others but to the social organization of the group, as indicated by the finding that productivity was related to clique membership and not to manual dexterity or intelligence.

Regularities do not occur accidentally. That official rules

[4] James Q. Wilson, *Varieties of Police Behavior* (Cambridge: Harvard University Press, 1968), pp. 220–222. Copyright, 1968, by the President and Fellows of Harvard College. By permission.

bring them about is expected, but what is the source of those regularities in social conduct that do not reflect official standards? They are also the result of normative standards, but standards that have emerged in the work group itself rather than having been officially instituted by superiors or formal blueprints. In the course of social interaction at work, there arise patterned expectations and norms, which find expression in a network of social relationships and in prevailing practices. As each worker in the Bank Wiring Observation Room grew accustomed to playing games with some coworkers and not with others, his role became socially defined as part of one of the two cliques, or of neither, and the group became structured accordingly. Simultaneously, there developed normative beliefs shared by all members of the group: "Don't be a rate-buster by working too fast!" "Don't be a chiseler by working too slowly!" "Don't act bossy!" "Don't be a squealer!" These unofficial standards governed the behavior of the workers. One inspector was excluded from both cliques, because he acted officiously and even reported other workers to superiors. Despite a complicated wage incentive system, some restriction of output existed. Since too fast as well as too slow work was condemned, wiremen did not try to produce as much as they could, although doing so would have increased their pay, but slacked their pace after they had completed what they considered to be "a fair day's work." Differences in output within this group would probably have been smaller if it had not been divided into two cliques. One of these emphasized that the worker should not produce too much, and the other, that he should not produce too little, so that the members of each clique enjoyed social support for working slower or faster, respectively, than those of the other.

To be effective, social norms must be enforceable. Unless a member of a formal organization conforms with its official regulations to a certain minimum degree, he will be expelled. The reverse of this statement is also true: unless expulsion is a serious threat, the prevalence of conformity cannot be assured. The individual's motivation to remain part of the organization makes him subject to its control. Salaried employees are more dependable than unpaid volunteers in large part because economic dependence is a reliable mechanism for interesting the members of the organization in keeping their positions. The same principle holds for the enforcement of unofficial norms. Whereas the work group does not have the power to remove one of its members from his job and deprive him of his income, it can ostracize him and thereby exclude him from genuine group membership. But for such exclusion to be a threat that discourages deviant tendencies, the individual must first wish to be included in the group. If a person did not care about maintaining congenial relations with his co-workers, being cold-shouldered by them would neither disconcert him nor deter him from disregarding their social norms; and for him it would be "their" norms rather than "ours."

This is the reason why the existence of social cohesion is so significant for work groups. Strong mutual ties between the members of a group make each interested in maintaining his position in the group. In this situation, unofficial norms can readily be enforced, and it is rarely necessary to resort to the extreme penalty of ostracism, since lesser sanctions suffice to sustain conformity. If an individual violates a norm highly valued by the other members of the group, they will become less friendly toward him; this is virtually an automatic reaction when somebody's behavior displeases us. Such a change in interpersonal relationships endangers the individual's standing in the group and induces him, if he is identified with the group, to refrain from similar violations in the future in order to regain the favor of his colleagues or, at least, to prevent his relations with them from deteriorating further. Another type of informal sanction can be termed "ostracism in miniature." When several members of a group together ridicule a colleague or express aggression against him in some other form because he has violated an unofficial norm, they furnish him with a brief but concentrated demonstration of the nature of ostracism by standing united in opposition to him alone. The extremely disagreeable experience of feeling isolated while witnessing the solidarity of others constitutes a powerful incentive to abandon deviant practices lest this temporary state become a permanent one.

The effective enforcement of unofficial standards of conduct in cohesive work groups has important implications for official operations. Many studies have found that the existence of cohesive bonds between co-workers is a prerequisite for high morale and optimum performance of duties,[5] but this does not mean that all norms that arise in cohesive work groups contribute to the accomplishment of official tasks. The group's own standards in the Bank Wiring Observation Room, for example, since they discouraged the fastest workers from producing at a maximum rate, lowered productivity (although these standards simultaneously encouraged the slowest workers to increase their output). On the other hand, the fact that an unofficial practice directly conflicts with official regulations does not necessarily signify that it is detrimental to operating efficiency. The practice of consulting colleagues in violation of an official rule in the government agency apparently improved efficiency in operations, and so did the informal patterns on the island air base that defied the Navy's formal codes.

Paradoxically, unofficial practices that are explicitly prohibited by official regulations sometimes further the achievement of organizational objectives. This crucial finding raises questions about the concept of "informal organization" and about bureaucratic efficiency. Social scientists often set up a dichotomy between the informal and the formal organization and attempt to place every observation

[5] See, for instance, Roethlisberger and Dickson, *op. cit.*, pp. 3–186; and Elton Mayo, *The Human Problems of an Industrial Civilization* (New York: Macmillan, 1933).

into one of these pigeonholes. This procedure can only be misleading, since the distinction is an analytical one: there is only one actual organization. When government agents make official decisions in the course of informal discussions, their conduct cannot meaningfully be classified as belonging to either the formal or the informal organization. Even when a factory employee worked more slowly than he otherwise might have in conformity with unofficial norms, his behavior was also influenced by the formal requirements to manufacture telephone equipment and to use certain production methods for this purpose. Official as well as unofficial standards, formal as well as informal social relations, affect the ways in which the daily operations in work groups become organized, but the result is *one* social organization in each work group, not two.

Bureaucratic Ideologies

Social processes in bureaucracies modify their structures and operations. Some of these processes make the organization more flexible and responsive to changing conditions, such as the informal modifications of formal procedures that emerge, but other bureaucratic processes engender rigidities and resistance to change. The popular stereotype of bureaucracy exaggerates the rigidity of formal organizations, but it is not without considerable basis in fact. One important organizational process that engenders rigidity (we shall see in Chapter 6 that there are others) is the tendency, in large bureaucracies, for organizational ideologies to develop that take precedence over original goals, distort perceptions, and typically create resistance to change by sanctifying the existing state of affairs. It should be emphasized that concern here is not with the pathologies of individual bureaucrats but rather with organizational processes that lead to the shaping of conduct by ideologies or myths instead of by initial objectives and external realities. An ideology may be confined to a particular organization and glorify its traditions; or it may pertain to administrative practice in general and be widely accepted in many organizations.

Glorifying Myths

Large organizations tend to develop distinctive ideologies that glorify them and their members and exaggerate their virtues. The myths surrounding the U.S. Marines are a typical example. Such ideologies serve useful functions for the organization, by creating a sense of purpose among its members, strengthening their commitment and loyalty, and spurring them to greater efforts in behalf of the organization. Particularly significant is the role of these beliefs in transforming a collectivity of individuals with their separate goals into a working organization—something that exists apart from its members, which shapes their behavior, and which has overriding purposes. Philip Selznick describes this process as follows:

> To create an institution we rely on many techniques for infusing day-to-day behavior with long-run meaning and purpose. One of the most important of these techniques is the elaboration of socially integrating myths. These are efforts to state, in the language of uplift and idealism, what is distinctive about the aims and methods of the enterprise. Successful institutions are usually able to fill in the formula, "What we are proud of around here is . . ." Sometimes, a fairly explicit institutional philosophy is worked out; more often a sense of mission is communicated in more indirect but no less significant ways. The assignment of high prestige to certain activities will itself help to create a myth, especially if buttressed by occasional explicit statements. The specific ways of projecting a myth are as various as communication itself. For creative leadership, it is not the communication of a myth that counts; rather, creativity depends on having the will and the insight to see the necessity of the myth, to discover a successful formu-

lation, and above all to create the organizational conditions that will sustain the ideals expressed.[6]

Myths or ideologies, then, are integral parts of most large organizations. Without them organizations are little more than conglomerates of individuals. The common value orientations that ideologies represent are what forge human beings into social units having common purposes. Such social units are as distinctive from each other as individuals are from other individuals. Think of the profound differences between the New Left and the Republicans, between China and South Africa, between Southern blacks twenty years ago and today. Social movements would not come into existence were it not for ideologies which mobilize members and motivate them to invest time and energy in the movement. The distinctive nature of societies derives in good part from their national ideologies, which help define their boundaries and contribute to their strength. Organizations, too, benefit from ideologies that glorify their traditions, since in their absence motivation lags, employees have less investment in the common enterprise, and the organization is in fact less of a unified social entity.

In addition to these functions, however, glorifying myths have serious dysfunctions in organizations. There is the danger—indeed, it is hardly avoidable—that these myths, by capturing the imagination of the organization members, distort their perspectives, blind them against realities, and set them on courses of action that are detrimental to the organization's objectives. Characteristic of such myths is the claim of a particular organization—or society or subunit of an organization—to be superior to others of its kind. A familiar example is found when university academicians believe their department to be, if not one of the best, at least the one with the most balanced view of the discipline. The junior author, when choosing among graduate schools, was

[6] Philip Selznick, *Leadership in Administration* (New York: Harper & Row, 1957), p. 151.

once given the following sales talk: "Department X teaches you only theory; you'll never learn how to do research. Y University? Dust-bowl empiricism. They don't know what an idea is. *Here* there is a combination of theory and empirical research." Glorifying myths extol the importance of the department and place it at the top of the prestige ladder, in disregard of reality. The extent of aggrandizement of departmental prestige is illustrated by the finding of one study that fully half the departments surveyed believed themselves to be among the top five in their disciplines.[7]

If such ideological distortions can be observed in universities, whose members are trained in and committed to the critical examination of ideas, they are likely to be still more prevalent in other types of organizations, be they branches of the government, like the U.S. Marines, or private firms, like U.S. Steel. "Ours is a superior organization, with a great tradition and outstanding leaders." Such glorifying myths may seem to be harmless self-deceptions, which raise esprit de corps and the devotion of members to the organization. However, the ideological elaborations of these myths, as already stated, can have serious detrimental consequences for the organization and the people under its influence. Because ideologies tend to glorify not only the organization itself but also the existing arrangements and institutions within it and its particular leaders, critical evaluation of organizational patterns and practices is discouraged, top executives are insulated from criticisms, and needed innovations are not introduced. The ideology justifies traditional methods, which are rarely questioned and which tend to be thought of first as the best ways and ultimately as sacred traditions that must not be tampered with. Thus, the U.S. Department of Defense has not had its budget carefully scrutinized in the past, and when former Secretary of De-

[7] Theodore Caplow and Reese McGee, *The Academic Marketplace* (New York: Basic Books, 1958), p. 104.

fense Robert McNamara instituted evaluation procedures to eliminate waste, his doing so did not endear him to military leaders. Nobody likes to have his practices, decisions, or authority questioned, but ideologies strongly reinforce and broaden this resistance to critical appraisals.

Bureaucratic ideologies are shared values which identify the entire membership with the traditional arrangements in an organization. As a result of this ideological identification, criticisms of existing arrangements are objectionable to members whose work is not directly involved as well as to those whose work is affected. Moreover, the common ideology stamps individuals who point out shortcomings of the traditional ways of doing things as deviants, whose failure to share the prevailing values makes them unworthy of respect. This tendency discourages individuals who detect shortcomings from voicing their opinions. Hence, although many members of an organization may be aware of certain problems and deficiencies, each may think that all others are satisfied with existing arrangements, and this state of pluralistic ignorance, as it has been called, prevents the information from becoming official knowledge. An important source of pluralistic ignorance is the power of hierarchical superiors to sanction those who dissent from official policy. It usually takes a crisis for people's true feelings to "come out from under the rocks." Events during the early stages of the Vietnam War illustrate the dynamics of pluralistic ignorance. Though many members of the Lyndon B. Johnson administration had personal doubts about the government's policy, few objected publicly until they were shocked by the Army's request for 200,000 additional combat troops in the spring of 1968.[8] More recently, it has been revealed that a number of officials were critical of the policy and even contemplated resigning at the time, but few spoke out because they felt no support from their col-

[8] Clark Clifford, "Vietnam Reappraisal," *Foreign Affairs*, 47 (1969), 601–622.

leagues. Pluralistic ignorance led the administration into believing that consensus existed on its policies when in fact it did not, and thereby reinforced the tendency toward escalation.

While a bureaucratic ideology creates commitments that benefit the organization, it simultaneously tends to suppress the critical reviews that are essential for organizational vitality. Unless this tendency is checked, ossification sets in and produces the stereotype of the inefficient bureaucracy. The conditions for preventing such rigidity, easily outlined in principle but difficult to maintain in practice, are recurrent critical appraisals of all existing arrangements from diverse perspectives and a readiness to take these criticisms seriously and to make the modifications indicated. As we have seen, a strong organizational ideology discourages serious questioning of traditional arrangements, and so does a highly centralized authority structure, particularly if the highest executive has been in his position for many years. Thus, such a powerful executive as J. Edgar Hoover, who has been director of the Federal Bureau of Investigation since it was established, is likely to be firmly committed to existing arrangements, many of which he himself has instituted, to resent suggestions for changes as implicit criticisms of himself, and to resist implementing the few suggestions that may nevertheless be forthcoming. In this situation, senior management tends to be insulated from criticisms of current policies and procedures by the staff. A new top manager is more likely than an old-timer to institute changes in the organization, as noted at the end of the last chapter, probably in part because his lack of vested interests in existing arrangements encourages subordinates to communicate critical appraisals to him. Although managerial turnover creates problems of adjustment, and although organizational ideologies serve useful functions, it would seem that bureaucratic ossification is most likely to be averted if executive turnover is fairly frequent and if organizational ideologies play a minor role.

The Myth of "Scientific Management"

In the early part of this century, an ideology concerning administrative practices developed which went under the label of "scientific management," and which influenced management in many industrial organizations. Scientific management has attempted to rationalize industrial production and administration by discovering and applying the most efficient methods of operations.[9] Time-and-motion studies are a well-known illustration of this approach: the motions required by the most skilled workers for performing a given task in the shortest possible time are determined, and these exact motions are taught to other workers. But, as a well-known industrial sociologist points out, "managerial technologists have been far more successful in demonstrating efficient procedures for maximum productivity than they have been in getting such procedures accepted by workers."[10] This failure of scientific management was the inevitable result of its assumption, most evident in "scientific" wage incentive systems, that rational economic interests alone govern the conduct of employees and of its neglect of social factors. To administer a social organization according to purely technical criteria of rationality is irrational because the nonrational aspects of social conduct are ignored.

From an abstract standpoint, the most rational method of effecting uniformity and coordination in a large organization would appear to be to devise efficient procedures for every task and to insist that they be strictly followed. In practice, however, such a system would not function effectively for several reasons. One is that it implicitly assumes that management is omniscient. No system of rules and

---

[9] See Frederick W. Taylor, *The Principles of Scientific Management* (New York: Harper & Brothers, 1911).

[10] Wilbert E. Moore, *Industrial Relations and the Social Order* (New York: Macmillan, 1947), p. 190.

supervision can be so finely spun that it anticipates all exigencies that may arise. Changes in external conditions create new administrative problems, and the very innovations introduced to solve them often have unanticipated consequences that produce further problems. For example, the interviewers in a public employment agency were evaluated on the basis of the number of applicants for jobs they interviewed per month. As jobs became scarce after World War II, interviewers, induced by this method of evaluation to work fast, tended to dismiss clients for whom jobs could not be located quickly. In the interest of effective employment services, it was necessary to discourage such tendencies. For this purpose, a new method of evaluation, based primarily on the number of applicants placed in jobs, was instituted. This innovation did motivate interviewers to exert greater efforts to find jobs for clients, but it also gave rise to competition for the slips of paper on which job openings were recorded, which interviewers sometimes even hid from one another. These competitive practices were naturally a new obstacle to efficient operations. In response to the emergent problem, the most cohesive group of interviewers developed cooperative norms and successfully suppressed competitive tendencies, with the result that productive efficiency increased.[11] Unless the members of the organization have the freedom and initiative to deal with operating problems as they come up, efficiency will suffer.

Moreover, some impediments to operating efficiency cannot be eradicated by official decree. This is the case with respect to the anxieties and feelings of *anomie* (a state of feeling isolated and disoriented) that often arise among the lower echelons of bureaucratic hierarchies. Informal relations in cohesive work groups reduce such disruptive tensions. But once cohesive groups exist in the bureaucracy, as we have seen, they will develop their own standards of

[11] See Blau, *op. cit.*, pp. 57–81.

conduct and enforce them among their members. Administrative efficiency cannot be served by ignoring the fact that the performance of individuals is affected by their relations with colleagues, but only by taking cognizance of the fact and attempting to create those conditions in the organization that lead to unofficial practices which further rather than hinder the achievement of its objectives.

Finally, in a democratic culture, where independence of action and equality of status are highly valued, detailed rules and close supervision are resented, and resentful employees are poorly motivated to perform their duties faithfully and energetically. A striking contrast exists between the rigorous discipline employees willingly impose upon themselves because they realize that their work requires strict operating standards, and their constant annoyance at being hamstrung by picayune rules that they experience as arbitrarily imposed upon them. The members of the federal agency discussed earlier, for instance, often objected to having to fill out forms precisely, as we all do, and to other minor internal rules. However, they freely accepted the much more stringent discipline of adhering strictly to legal regulations in their investigations, which was necessitated by law enforcement itself. To repress the ability for self-imposed discipline and to undermine the motivation to exert efforts by prescribing in detail how every task is to be performed is wasteful, to say the least. A more efficient method of bureaucratic administration is to channel this ability and motivation to serve the ends of the organization.

Let us conclude this discussion with a reexamination of the concept of bureaucracy. Bureaucracies can be defined as formally established organizations designed to maximize administrative efficiency. In other words, they are characterized by formalized procedures for mobilizing and coordinating the collective efforts of many, usually specialized, individuals and subgroups in the pursuit of organizational objectives. However, social processes arise within the formal structure that modify it. Although the formally established structure and procedures are designed to further efficiency, some of these emergent processes defeat the formal design and create bureaucratic rigidity which interferes with adaptation to changing conditions and impedes efficiency. Other internal processes have the opposite effect and create informal adjustments to new situations and problems that arise, thus furthering effective operations. A fundamental dilemma of bureaucratic administration is that the very arrangements officially instituted to improve efficiency often have by-products that impede it. Centralized authority, even if it results in superior decisions, undermines the ability of middle managers to assume responsibilities. Detailed rules, even if they improve performance, prevent adaptation to changing situations. Strict discipline, even if it facilitates managerial direction, creates resentments that reduce effort. Generally, there are no formal arrangements that can assure efficiency because it depends on flexible adjustments to varying and changing conditions in the organization. What formal arrangements can and should do, however, is create conditions in the organization that foster processes of adjustment. The main task of management is not to lay down rules on how to do the work but to maintain conditions in which adjustments spontaneously occur when new problems arise and to protect these conditions from bureaucratic processes of ossification.

4

Bureaucratic Authority

The hierarchy of authority in a bureaucracy, though essential for coordination, often produces among its lower echelons profound feelings of dissatisfaction and apathy which impede identification with the organization's objectives. Effective operations suffer unless a method of hierarchical coordination develops that minimizes these harmful consequences for work motivation. The analysis of bureaucratic authority and the dilemmas it creates is the topic of this chapter.

Let us start with one of these dilemmas of bureaucratic authority—a conflict between official requirements and actual practice. In theory, bureaucratic superiors are expected to exercise strict and impersonal control over subordinates. But in fact, first-line supervisors and foremen frequently "play ball" with their subordinates and let them "get away with" infractions of many rules. What accounts for this leniency?

Strategic Leniency and Authority

A psychological explanation of the failure to enforce strict discipline among subordinates might attribute it to poor leadership. Some supervisors are overly lenient, it could be held, because inborn or acquired personality traits prevent them from asserting their authority over others and maintaining effective leadership. Note that this explanation assumes as a matter of course that the bureaucratic superior who appears lenient merely indulges his subordinates and is less effective than the disciplinarian in discharging his supervisory responsibilities. Empirical evidence, however, indicates that the very opposite is often true.

A study of twenty-four clerical sections in an insurance company analyzed the relationship between method of supervision and productive efficiency.[1] In closely supervised sections, whose heads gave clerks detailed instructions and frequently checked up on them, productivity was usually lower than in sections where employees were given more freedom to do the work in their own way. Moreover, supervisors who were primarily concerned with maintaining a high level of production, interestingly enough, were less successful in meeting this goal than those supervisors who were more interested in the welfare of their subordinates than in sheer production; in the latter case, productivity was generally higher. Finally, groups who worked under more authoritarian supervisors were, on the whole, less productive than those supervised in a relatively democratic fashion. Other studies have also found that disciplinarian supervisors are less effective than more liberal ones.[2]

Such findings are often misinterpreted as signifying that

[1] Daniel Katz, Nathan Maccoby, and Nancy C. Morse, *Productivity, Supervision and Morale in an Office Situation* (Ann Arbor: Institute for Social Research, University of Michigan, 1950), especially pp. 17, 21, 29.
[2] See, for instance, F. J. Roethlisberger and William J. Dickson, *Management and the Worker* (Cambridge: Harvard University Press, 1946), pp. 452–453.

democratic ways are superior to authoritarian ones. But this is a rather loose use of the term "democratic," the exact meaning of which is worth preserving. Since "democracy" denotes rule from below (literally, "people's rule") and not from above, one person's supervision of others cannot, by definition, be democratic. This is not the place for a discussion of the relationship between democracy and bureaucracy; the final chapter is reserved for this purpose. But here it should be noted that tolerant supervisory practices, in contrast to disciplinarian ones, are neither democratic nor an indication that controlling power over subordinates has been surrendered. On the contrary, leniency in supervision is a potent strategy, consciously or unconsciously employed, for establishing authority over subordinates, and this is the reason why the liberal supervisor is particularly effective.

Let us clarify the concept of authority. First, it refers to a relationship between persons and not to an attribute of one individual. Second, authority involves exercise of social control which rests on the *willing* compliance of subordinates with certain directives of the superior. He need not coerce or persuade subordinates in order to influence them, because they have accepted as legitimate the principle that some of their actions should be governed by his decisions. Third, authority is an observable pattern of interaction and not an official definition of a social relationship. If a mutinous crew refuses to obey the captain's orders, he does not in fact have authority over his men. Whatever the superior's official rights to command obedience and the subordinates' official duties to obey him, his authority over them extends only to conduct that they voluntarily permit to be governed by his directives. Actual authority, consequently, is not granted by the formal organizational chart, but must be established in the course of social interaction, although the official bureaucratic structure, as we shall see presently, facilitates its establishment.

What are some of the practices of a lenient foreman or supervisor? Above all, he allows subordinates to violate minor rules, to smoke or talk, for example, despite the fact that it is prohibited by management. This permissiveness often increases his power over them by furnishing him with legitimate sanctions that he can use as he sees fit. If an action of his subordinates displeases him, the superviser can punish them by commanding: "Cut out the smoking! Can't you read the sign?" Had he always enforced the rule, this penalty would not have been available to him. Indeed, so crude a use of sanctions is rarely necessary. The mere knowledge that the rule exists and, possibly, that it is enforced elsewhere, instills a sense of obligation to liberal superiors and induces subordinates more readily to comply with their requests.

Whereas the disciplinarian supervisor generally asserts his official prerogatives, the lenient and relaxed one does not. The latter attempts to take the wishes of his subordinates into account in arranging their work schedule, although he has the right to assign their work at his own discretion. Sometimes he goes to special trouble to accommodate a subordinate. Instead of issuing curt commands, he usually explains the reasons for his directives. He calls his subordinates by their first names and encourages their use of his first name (especially in democratically minded American organizations). When one of his subordinates gets into difficulties with management, he is apt to speak up for him and to defend him. These different actions have two things in common: the superior is not required to do them, and his subordinates welcome his doing them. Such conduct therefore creates social obligations. To repay the supervisor for past favors, and not to risk the cessation of similar favors in the future, subordinates voluntarily comply with many of his requests, including some they are not officially required to obey. By refraining from exercising his power of control whenever it is legitimate to do so, the bureaucratic superior establishes effective authority over subordinates, which enables him to control them much more effectively than otherwise would be possible.

Complementary role expectations arise in the course of interaction between superior and subordinates and become crystallized in the course of interaction among subordinates. As the superior permits subordinates to violate some rules and to make certain decisions themselves, and as they grow accustomed to conforming with many of his directives, they learn to expect to exercise discretion in some areas and to follow supervisory directives in others, and he learns to expect this pattern of conduct from them. The members of the work group, by watching one another at work and talking among themselves about the manner in which they perform their duties, develop social consensus about these role expectations and thereby reinforce them. The newcomer to the group, who must be taught "how things are done around here" as distinguished from "what's in the book," provides an opportunity for further affirming this consensus by making it explicit.

The resulting common role expectations are often so fully internalized that employees are hardly aware of being governed by them. The members of one department might find it natural for their supervisor to interrupt their work and tell them to start on a new task. The members of another department in the same organization might consider such a supervisory order as gross interference with their work, since they had become accustomed to using their discretion about the sequence of their tasks, yet readily comply with other directives of the supervision. These role expectations of independence from the supervisor in some areas and unquestioning obedience in others define the limits of his authority over subordinates.

Power of Sanction

The preceding comments apply to informal leadership as well as to bureaucratic authority. The informal leader, like the prudent bureaucratic superior, establishes his authority over his followers by creating social obligations.[3] Once a relationship of authority exists, both bureaucratic superior and informal leader can afford to word their orders as mere suggestions, because even these are readily followed by the rest of the group. Neither of them usually needs sanctions to command obedience, though sanctions are available to both of them in case they wish to use special inducements, since praise or blame of the person in the superordinate position itself exerts a powerful influence.

Nevertheless, there is a fundamental distinction between informal leadership and bureaucratic authority. Informal leadership freely emerges among a group of peers. It is initially the result of personality differences that have become socially magnified. Some members of the group excel in activities that are highly valued by all, whether these are street fighting or solving complex problems; these few will be more respected, and their opinions will carry greater weight. The person in the extreme position, if he also finds ways to obligate the others to him, is expected to be the group's leader.

Bureaucratic authority, on the other hand, prevents the group itself from conferring the position of leadership upon the member of their choice. The voluntary obedience of subordinates must converge upon the individual officially placed in the position of supervisor, irrespective of his personal characteristics. The bureaucratic mechanism that makes this state of affairs a predictable occurrence is the superior's power to impose sanctions, typically in the form of ratings of the performance of his subordinates, which influence their chances of advancement and of keeping their jobs.

The dependency of bureaucratic subordinates upon their immediate superior produced by his rating power engenders

---

[3] For a clear illustration of this point in a street corner gang, see William F. Whyte, *Street Corner Society* (Chicago: University of Chicago Press, 1943), pp. 257-262.

frustrations and anxieties for adults. It forces employees to worry about their supervisor's reaction at every step they take. An effective way to weaken or avoid such feelings is to identify with the bureaucratic system of normative standards and objectives. By making this system a part of their own thinking, employees transform conformity with its principles from submission to the superior's demands into voluntary action. Guided by internalized standards, they are less likely to experience external restraints in performing their duties. Moreover, once the hierarchical division of responsibility has been accepted as a basic principle of the organization, it becomes less threatening to a person's self-esteem to obey the supervisor's directives, since he is known to be duty-bound to issue them, just as it is not degrading to obey the traffic directions of a policeman. Dependence on the superior's rating encourages the adoption of a bureaucratic orientation, for the disadvantages of dependence can thereby be evaded.

It is of crucial importance that this process of identification with bureaucratic standards does not occur in isolation but in a social situation. All members of the work group find themselves in the same position of dependence on their supervisor. (In fact, all members of the bureaucratic organization are, in varying degrees, dependent on their immediate superiors.) Together, they can obtain concessions from the supervisor, because he is anxious to obligate them by granting some of their demands. In exchange, they feel constrained to comply with many of his directives. Typically, a strict definition is given to the limits of this effective authority. Subordinates can often be heard to remark: "That's the supervisor's responsibility. He gets paid for making those decisions." This does not mean that operating employees shirk responsibilities, as indicated by their willingness to shoulder those they define as their own. But the social agreement among the members of the work group that making certain decisions and issuing certain directives is the duty of the supervisor, not merely his privilege, serves to emphasize that following them does not constitute submission to his arbitrary will but conformity with commonly accepted operating principles. In such a situation, which prevails in some organizations though by no means in all, subordinates do not experience the supervisor's exercise of authority over them as domination; neither are they necessarily envious of his responsibilities, since they frequently consider their own more challenging than his.

The effective establishment of authority obviates the need for sanctions in daily operations. If a supervisor commands the voluntary obedience of subordinates, he need not induce them to obey him by promising them rewards or threatening them with punishment. In fact, the use of sanctions undermines authority. A supervisor who is in the habit of invoking sanctions to back his orders—"You won't get a good rating unless you do this!"—shows that he does not expect unqualified compliance. As subordinates learn that he does not expect it, they will no longer feel obligated unconditionally to accept his directives. Moreover, employees resent being continually reminded of their dependence on the supervisor by his promises and threats, and such resentment makes them less inclined to carry out his orders.

This is the dilemma of bureaucratic authority: it rests on the power of sanction but is weakened by frequent resort to sanctions in operations. A basic difference, however, should be noted between the periodic rating of the performance of subordinates, which can be called a *diffuse sanction*, and *specific sanctions* recurrently employed to enforce particular commands. Since all employees know that their immediate superior is officially required to evaluate their operations at periodic intervals, this evaluation is neither a sign that he does not expect unqualified compliance with his directives nor a reason for annoyance with him. This diffuse sanction, imposed only annually or every few months, creates the dependence of subordinates upon their supervisor but does not constantly endanger their willingness to be guided by his requests, as the habitual use of specific sanctions (including promises of good ratings and threats of poor ones) would.

While the mere fact that the supervisor administers ratings is not resented by his subordinates, low ratings might well antagonize some of them. But bureaucratic mechanisms exist that enable the supervisor to shift the blame for negative sanctions. For example, statistical records of performance, which are kept in many white-collar offices as well as factories, furnish the supervisor with objective evidence with which he can justify low ratings by showing the recipients that the poor quality of their work left him no other choice. Instead of blaming the supervisor for giving them a poor rating, these employees are forced to blame themselves or to attribute the rating to the "statistics," which are often accused, rightly or wrongly, of failing to measure the qualitative aspects of performance.[4]

His intermediate position in the hierarchy provides the supervisor with another justification mechanism. He can place the responsibility for giving low ratings or instituting unpopular requirements on his superiors, to whom he is accountable. Oftentimes a supervisor or foreman will tell his subordinates that he does not like certain standards any better than they do but "those brass-hats in the front office" insist on them. In most organizations, one or a few superintendents or assistant managers (or deans) become the scapegoats who are blamed for negative sanctions and unpopular requirements. Since the attitudes of employees toward these administrators in removed positions are much less relevant for effective operations than their attitudes toward their immediate superior, the displacement of aggression from him to them is in the interest of the organization. Clients or customers can also serve as scapegoats of aggression—the supervisor can blame their demands for instituting procedures that inconvenience employees. And if he joins sub-

---

[4] Of course, quantitative records also facilitate the supervisor's task of evaluating operations.

ordinates in ridiculing clients or customers, a frequent practice in service occupations, the supervisor further reduces antagonism against himself by standing united with the employees against outsiders.

Performance ratings, then, increase the dependency of the members of a bureaucracy on their superiors but at the same time allow them to escape from disturbing feelings of dependency by internalizing the principles that govern operations. Although the responsibilities the supervisor is required to discharge occasionally arouse the animosity of some subordinates, various mechanisms divert such antagonism from the supervisor to other objects. These two elements of the bureaucratic structure conspire to provide a fertile soil for the establishment of supervisory authority. Together, they permit supervisors to obligate subordinates willingly to follow directives.

Various circumstances, however, can prevent such favorable conditions in the bureaucratic organization. The disciplinarian supervisor may antagonize subordinates, through recurrent use of sanctions and in other ways, and thereby undermine his effective authority over them as well as their motivation to put effort into their work. The lenient supervisor may be so reluctant to displease subordinates that he refrains from evaluating their performance in accordance with rigorous standards, giving all of them high ratings. This practice invalidates the incentive system, which enhances the interest of employees in accomplishing specified results in their operations. The manipulative supervisor may employ devious techniques to conceal from subordinates his attempts to impose his arbitrary will upon them, for example, by frequent and unwarrented utilization of scapegoats. While manipulative techniques have a fair chance of being successful in temporary pair relationships, as between customer and salesman, their chances of success in relatively permanent relationships within a group are very slim. For sooner or later, some member is apt to see through them, and he is not likely to keep this a secret. Once they are discovered, manipulative techniques have a boomerang effect. Employees who realize that their superior tries to manipulate them are prone to suspect all of his statements and generally to resist his efforts to influence their performance.

These and other disruptive tendencies can be observed in hierarchical organizations, but methods of supervision that encourage operating efficiency are also evident. In the absence of a much larger body of information about bureaucracies than we now possess, it is impossible to know which of these opposite conditions is more frequent. Nevertheless, the fact that authority is sometimes effectively exercised without domineering subordinates or lowering their morale, rare as this may be, demonstrates that such a state of affairs is actually possible and not merely a utopian ideal type.

Authority of Office and Authority of Expertness

Traditional bureaucracies assume that just as gradations of hierarchy correspond to levels of authority, they also correspond to degrees of competence. Supervisors are considered more expert than their subordinates, and the boss, in addition to possessing managerial skills, is assumed to have more *technical* knowledge than anyone else in the organization. Expertness and hierarchical authority are not distinguished but are presumed identical. Advances in technology and the increasing use of specialized experts in organizations have rendered this assumption a shambles as managers are forced to hire people whose work they do not understand and whose competencies they cannot evaluate.

Victor A. Thompson finds this problem critical in understanding relationships between line employees and staff members in bureaucracies, but his analysis can be extended to the general case of relationships between experts and nonexperts in organizational settings.

Advancing specialization upsets status expectations as well as vested interests in functions. Specialization, by giving a function to everyone, brings low- and high-status persons into interdependent relationships, thereby violating the status expectations of the latter.

The "staff" threat to function and status is particularly acute with regard to hierarchial, or "line" positions low enough down to contain specialist content. In fact, the conflict arising from these new specialties is usually designated as the line-staff conflict. Since specialties eventually win legitimacy one way or another, they acquire authority of a non-hierarchial kind which invades the domain of hierarchial authority. In this way there arises a growing discrepancy between *expected authority* and *actual authority* which lies at the heart of the line-staff conflict. . . . Here we wish only to call attention to the universally adopted devices of derogating staff importance ("Line is more important than staff.") and of attempting to suppress recognition of the unpalatable features of the relationship by the use of fictions ("Staff only advises; it does not command.").[5]

The placement of experts alongside nonexperts creates potential for conflict, but more important, it generates professional competence as a basis for authority which traditional theories of organization do not recognize.[6] For the observer, this introduces ambiguities, for authority no longer resides solely in offices but is instead derived from the qualifications people bring to their jobs. Tables of organization do not anticipate the day-to-day patterns of work relationships as well as they once did, and the notion that "final authority" over any particular matter rests in a

[5] Victor A. Thompson, *Modern Organization* (New York: Knopf, 1961), pp. 100–101. Copyright © 1961 by Victor A. Thompson.
[6] For discussions of professional authority, see Talcott Parsons, *The Social System* (Glencoe, Ill.: Free Press, 1951), pp. 428–479; the same author's introduction to Max Weber, *The Theory of Social and Economic Organization*, translated by A. M. Henderson and Talcott Parsons (New York: Oxford University Press, 1947), pp. 58–59, *n.* 4; and Alvin W. Gouldner, *Patterns of Industrial Bureaucracy* (Glencoe, Ill.: Free Press, 1954), pp. 21–23.

specified office becomes little more than fiction. For the manager, the authority of experts also creates ambiguities, for he is confronted by a group comprised of people who are nominally his subordinates, but whose special expertness allows them to dispute his judgment. Given that the presence of experts at a low level of an organization creates uncertainties in the command structure, it might be tempting for executives to assert or reassert the authority of their offices to buttress hierarchical control. But this course has its costs, too, and they may be greater than whatever is lost by relaxing the assumption that there is one and only one "line of authority."

A refusal to let go of traditional prerogatives and to recognize that authority inheres in expertness as well as in offices has some unanticipated consequences. Perhaps its most insidious effect is the development of covert power relationships between expert and nonexpert employees. The power of experts when it is neither legitimate nor officially recognized (whereas authority always is)becomes manifest in periods of uncertainty or crisis when their services are in great demand. This pattern detracts from an organization's efficiency, for it is in the interest of experts to maintain the uncertainty that makes them indispensable and to withhold as much of their expert knowledge as they can, particularly from their hierarchical superiors.

Expertness as a Source of Power

In a study of the French tobacco monopoly, Michel Crozier observed that maintenance men wielded considerably more influence than the supervisors of production workers. Crozier notes that the rigidities of the French bureaucratic system are in part responsible for this. Since the duties, rights, and prerogatives of officials are spelled out in detail in elaborate codes, supervisors have little discretion, and their subordinates know exactly what to expect of them. The one thing that cannot be anticipated and for which no codified procedures exist is machine breakdown. When stoppages occur, a maintenance worker must be called, and the repair and restoration of production are entirely in his hands. The result is as follows:

> There remains one group relationship with all the connotations of dependency and attendant emotional feelings. This is the relationship between the maintenance workers and the production workers. We must try to understand how it has come about and how it relates to the system as a whole.
>
> This relationship is centered around the problems of machine stoppages. Machine stoppages occur unusually often because of the difficulties in conditioning the raw material. This is a sore spot in the technological system. However, comparable problems seem to be handled better in other factories in France, and in similar factories working with the same technology in other countries. Elsewhere, at least, they are not considered the crucial events they have become in the Monopoly.
>
> There are apparently two complementary reasons for their being crucial in the bureaucratic organizational setup of the Monopoly. First, machine stoppages are the only major happenings that cannot be predicted and to which impersonal rulings cannot apply. The rules govern the consequences of the stoppages, the reallocation of jobs, and the adjustment of the work load and of pay; but they cannot indicate when the stoppage will occur and how long it will last. The contrast between the detailed rigidity of all other prescribed behavior and the complete uncertainty of mechanical functioning gives this problem disproportionate importance. Second, the people who are in charge of maintenance and repair are the only ones who can cope with machine stoppage. They cannot be overseen by anyone in the shop. No one can understand what they are doing and check on them. Furthermore, a department—a rather abstract service unit—is not responsible. Instead, men are individually responsible, each of them for a number of machines. Thus there is another contrast between impersonality and abstractness on the one side, and individual responsibility on the other.
>
> Production workers are displeased by the consequences of

machine stoppage. It disrupts their work; it is likely to make it necessary for them to work harder to compensate for lost time; and if it lasts long enough, they will be displaced, losing friendship ties and even status.

With machine stoppages, a general uncertainty about what will happen next develops in a world totally dominated by the value of security. It is not surprising, therefore, that the behavior of the maintenance man—the man who alone can handle the situation, and who by preventing these unpleasant consequences gives workers the necessary security—has tremendous importance for production workers, and that they try to please him and he to influence them. From this state of affairs, a power relationship develops.

The contrast between the power wielded by the maintenance men and the lack of influence of the supervisors explains the advantage that the former have over the latter. Supervisors cannot check on maintenance. They may be competent in the various aspects of their work, but their competence does not extend to the only problem about which the workers care, because only its outcome is uncertain. A supervisor cannot reprimand the mechanics who work in his shop. There is likely to be a perpetual fight for control, and the supervisors will usually be the losers. It is, therefore, natural for them to have low morale, and to adjust to their situation only after having resigned themselves to being the losers—using whatever rationalization they please.

Maintenance workers, on the other hand, have the best of this situation; but their power is contested. It is not an overt, legitimate power. It does not fit the usual expectations of industrial leadership. As a result, maintenance workers still feel insecure. One can understand that their aggressiveness is a way of warding off any attack, of cementing the group solidarity and making individual compromise impossible. It is a value necessary to group struggle—and effective in it. Soul-searching and moderation are qualities the group will definitely refuse to consider; and these qualities tend to make people marginal, if not outcasts.

Production workers resent their dependence, but cannot express their hostility openly, because they need the maintenance men's help and good will individually at the shop, and because, collectively, they know that they can keep their privileges only by maintaining a common front with the other workers' group. Union solidarity and working-class unity are the values in the names of which production workers accept the maintenance workers' leadership. These values are important to them, because of their feelings of insecurity. They feel that they have rights and privileges that are not customary in the usual industrial setups in France, and that they must protect themselves. They fear that they will not be able to keep these assets unless they are prepared to fight. Since the production workers are in this state of mind, the threats of abandoning them which maintenance men make are always successful.

The system of organization we have described may appear quite unworkable. Groups fight endlessly. It seems that there is no way of making changes and adjusting to new conditions. The system appears completely static. Yet it works, with a low but adequate degree of efficiency, and it has incorporated, in one way or another, every stage of technological progress.[7]

Crozier concludes that control over uncertainty is an important source of power in organizations. Since experts are by definition more knowledgeable and skilled than nonexperts, one would expect them to have an advantage over others in uncertain situations. The dilemma facing managers is whether or not to recognize this advantage and give it legitimacy. If they do, their own hierarchical authority is compromised, but if they do not, crises and informal power struggles will be endemic.

A Note on Collegiality

In the professions and academic disciplines, authority is often exercised by groups of colleagues rather than individual supervisors and directors. Promotion to a tenured

---

[7] Michel Crozier, *The Bureaucratic Phenomenon* (Chicago: University of Chicago Press, 1964), pp. 108–110. Copyright 1964 by the University of Chicago. Reprinted by permission of the author and the University of Chicago Press.

position, for example, usually requires the approval of the majority of senior professors in a department. In some professional groups, misconduct cases are heard by committees on ethics elected by the membership. Collegial authority exists in place of hierarchical authority for several reasons. Many members of the professions, especially the traditional ones of medicine, law, and the ministry, are solo practitioners who have no bosses, and professors might just as well be because they usually teach and do research without supervision. The complexities of evaluation make it all the more difficult for an individual professional to hold authority over others. A surgeon's skill, a lawyer's competence, and a scholar's research are not easily judged, and there may be sharp disagreements about a man's work. The existence of broad professional norms—protection of one's client, disinterestedness, commitment to the truth—in place of specific rules further confuses matters.

Collegial authority does not exist in a vacuum, however. Like hierarchical authority, it is exercised through organizations—professional societies and academic disciplines. But unlike settings where there is a designated superior, professional and academic groups develop ideals to which members are meant to conform and thus, *as groups*, exercise authority over members. Professionals in administrative roles, of course, have prerogatives based on their offices; and as practitioners or teachers, their authority is derived from expertness. However, the way a professional exercises authority over other professionals (which is the constant dilemma of the hospital or academic administrator) or over clients or students is regulated by standards set by his colleagues.

5

The Comparative
Study of Organizations

Bureaucracy is studied in a number of different ways by
social scientists. Organizations can be treated as contexts in
which much of human behavior takes place; the focus is
upon individual persons and their interaction rather than
upon bureaucracy as such. To study the effects of group
discussions on attitudes, one might well want to use employees of a large organization as subjects and to design an
experiment in which they discuss impending changes in
work procedures. The results of such experiments—in one
such case it was shown that discussions do diminish resistance to change[1]—contribute to knowledge of group processes and are useful for facilitating organizational change.
The study of the effects of different styles of supervision on
employees' performances is another illustration of research

[1] Lester Coch and John French, Jr., "Overcoming Resistance to
Change," in Eleanor E. Maccoby, Theodore M. Newcomb, and
Eugene L. Hartley (eds.), *Readings in Social Psychology*, 3rd ed.
(New York: Holt, Rinehart and Winston, 1958), pp. 233–250.

focused on the individual within the organization. It has been found that most people resent close supervision; old-fashioned bossism does not appear to contribute to organizational effectiveness.[2]

Bureaucracy can also be studied in order to understand the structure of large organizations. The term "organizational structure" refers to properties of organizations that are *not* characteristics of their members, notably, properties of the distribution of social positions in the organization. For instance, we can speak of the division of labor in an organization (or in a whole society), but the concept cannot be applied to individual persons. Similarly, a hierarchy of authority occurs in organizations but is not a characteristic of individuals. A man has a job title and a rank in the hierarchy, but it is only the *relationships* among jobs or ranks that comprise the division of labor or the hierarchy of authority. Bureaucratic rules and regulations, while not part of the status structure, are likewise properties of organizations.

The structure of organizations is of interest to social scientists for more than one reason. Some theorists, especially Emile Durkheim, recommended that sociology confine itself to studying phenomena other than individual behavior, such as the impact of social integration on what he called "suicidal currents at the societal level." In practice, however, most sociological research has considered largely variables describing individuals—attitudes, behavior, and demographic characteristics, including age, sex, years of education, and so forth. The study of organizational structure follows Durkheim's approach and is primarily concerned with aspects of social structure that are properties of organizations—firms, government agencies, hospitals—and that usually have no individual-level counterparts. Another reason for investigating organizational structure is to pro-

[2] Robert L. Kahn and Daniel Katz, "Leadership Practices in Relation to Productivity and Morale," in Dorwin Cartwright and Alvin Zander (eds.), *Group Dynamics: Research and Theory*, 2nd ed. (New York: Harper & Row, 1962), pp. 527–553.

vide answers to questions raised by students of bureaucracy: What are the conditions that give rise to a complex hierarchy of authority? Do detailed rules and regulations contribute to centralization or decentralization of control? What is the impact of automation and other technological advances on the way work is organized and authority is distributed?

Dimensions of Analysis

It may be convenient to distinguish three dimensions of analysis that are commonly used in studying bureaucracy. The first might be called the *role dimension*. At this level, concern is primarily with the characteristics and behavior of individuals in their roles as members of organizations. For example, when the relationship of job satisfaction to productivity is considered, we need only information about individual workers—how each likes his job, and how much he is producing.

The second level of analysis might be called the *group dimension* (though sometimes the term "structural" is used). Here we are interested in the influence of one or more person's activities on the behavior of other people and generally in the social processes that govern the informal organization in work groups. To examine whether cooperative or competitive work groups are more productive, for example, information about these groups themselves is most appropriate. One might want to know how many competitive persons there are in each group, and how their presence affects the output of less competitive members. It has been found that while competitive workers themselves are most productive, their presence tends to decrease the output of others.

A third level of analysis is the *organizational dimension*. At this level, attention centers on characteristics of whole organizations, not of individuals or work groups. When one asks what form of organization is most conducive to efficient operations—for example, whether centralization or decentralization is—he is thinking of organizations as wholes, not of the individual members or the work groups that comprise them. A manager may divide work by purpose instead of by process, or he may decide to decrease the size of the administrative staff, as a possible means of increasing organizational effectiveness. In both cases, he is concerned with the *structure* of his organization. The organizational dimension of analysis, then, focuses on properties of formal organizations, which are typically so large that all members do not interact with, and in many cases do not even know, one another.

The three dimensions of analysis focus attention upon different problems in the study of organizational life. Role analysis is appropriate if we are interested in studying how existing conditions in bureaucracies affect the attitudes and behavior of their individual members—for example, what conditions improve work satisfaction, whether work satisfaction enhances productivity, or which bureaucratic pressures lead to rigid overconformity. Group analysis is the proper focus if we are concerned with clarifying the informal organization of work groups and the ways in which the interpersonal relations among colleagues affect performance, as we were in Chapter 3. Both of these approaches take the existing characteristics of organizations as given and examine their implications for internal social processes and for the groups and individual members in these organizations. But if what we want to know is why organizations develop certain characteristics and how other characteristics affect the development of these—for instance, how size and complexity affect the authority structure—we must resort to organizational analysis, which focuses attention on the variations in organizational attributes among bureaucracies, and which consequently can seek answers to the question of why some organizations have different characteristics from others.

Organizational analysis is carried out on the basis of the

comparative study of several, and often large numbers, of organizations, whereas the two other approaches usually employ case studies. Before the differences between the comparative and the case study of organizations are examined, a few remarks are in order about the concepts used in organizational analysis. Many of the concepts of sociology and social psychology, such as social class, group cohesion, and cultural values, derive their meaning not only from exact definitions but also from the understanding our personal experience provides. We are all familiar with class differences. It is our experience in more or less well-knit groups that conveys to us the meaning of group cohesion. As soon as we set foot into another culture, or even read about it, we realize the profound significance traditional values have upon social life. But most attributes of organizations are more abstract than these and further removed from everyday experience. Individuals have experience with working in more or less specialized jobs, but not with differences in the degree of the division of labor in an organization, which is not the same thing. (In a specialized organization, most employees may have highly specialized jobs, yet there may be little division of labor among them.) Whereas individuals experience how authoritarian their boss is, several aspects of the authority structure are not directly experienced, such as the number of levels in the hierarchy, or how this number affects the span of control of managers—that is, the number of subordinates per manager. Since many of the concepts used in organizational analysis are not readily understood in terms of personal experience, it is particularly important to define them precisely. To say we want to study the authority structure and how the size of organizations influences it is not enough. We must specify what variations in the authority structure are of interest—for example, vertical differentiation, horizontal differentiation, and decentralization of responsibilities—and we must find empirical measures for these concepts.

Methods in Studying Organizational Structure

A variety of methods exists for studying organizational structure. One can use a case study or comparative research on a large number of organizations, and one can employ quantitative as well as qualitative procedures. Case studies of organizations are not necessarily qualitative; similarly, comparative research on organizations does not necessarily involve quantification.

The term "comparative" needs some explanation. The reader may be familiar with its use in research on politics. There, "comparative" means cross-national: the research concerns two or more countries. Comparative research on organizations can also be cross-national. One could, for instance, study Sears Roebuck in Lima, Peru, and Sears Roebuck in Schenectady, New York, and call this a comparative study. But while the comparative study of national political systems must be international, because each country has only one, the comparative study of organizations does not have to be, because there are many organizations in every country. Hence, one can conduct a comparative study of Sears Roebuck stores, or other firms, within the United States. The objective would be to make systematic comparisons and try to explain the differences. The principle of comparative analysis, then, is the study of two or more social structures. In political research, the relevant structures are usually nation-states, though they could be parties. In organizational research, the relevant structures are organizations, whether or not they are in different countries. Thus, when we speak of comparative studies of organizations, we are referring to research on a number of organizations. The research may include only a few contrasting cases or sufficient numbers to permit quantitative analysis, though there is a trend toward quantification in studies of organization. Not all quantitative studies are comparative ones, on the other hand. Systematic observations or surveys of members' attitudes may yield rigorous quantitative data, but as long as the procedures are confined to one organization, the investigation remains a case study.

Let us contrast the data obtainable and the research strategies employed in comparative and in case studies of organizations, and examine the advantages and limitations of either method.

Case studies incorporate a wealth of data about one organization. While the investigator is often interested in one or two broad problems, the range of variables to be included in a case study is not usually delimited in advance. It is thus possible to gather additional information continually as new variables become important in analysis and interpretation. In the Hawthorne research, for example, no one initially thought that the *social* conditions of work were important for productivity. Only after the discovery that opposite changes in such physical conditions as illumination had the same effect of raising productivity, despite the fact that at one point, "the amount of light [was] approximately equal to that on an ordinary moonlight night,"[3] was it realized that the experiments themselves had altered the workers' social situations and feelings about their jobs. The focus of the Hawthorne studies then shifted to the social relations in the work situations and their significance for productivity and morale. Comparative studies, by contrast, include relatively few data describing each of a large number of organizations. Since data for comparative studies are often gathered from structured interviews with informants or from published sources, the range of variables to be considered must be fixed in advance. The researcher with limited resources will usually not be able to return to the set of organizations later in order to collect more information about them.

Case study methods do not require the investigator to

[3] Fritz Roethlisberger and William J. Dickson, *Management and the Worker* (Cambridge: Harvard University Press, 1939), p. 17.

specify detailed hypotheses in advance. He may have a tentative list of propositions he wishes to test, but these can be modified and reformulated in the course of the research. Conclusions are reached by observing sequences of events and imputing a causal nexus to them. For instance, if it is noted that a manager, because of his lack of informal personal ties with employees, devises bureaucratic regulations as a means of securing compliance with his directives, it is argued that managerial succession may generally foster bureaucratization. If the introduction of statistical records of performance is followed by a change of the supervisor's role from boss to consultant, the generalization is inferred that impersonal mechanisms of control tend to improve supervisor-subordinate relationships.

In comparative studies of organizations, relationships among organizational characteristics are established either by contrasting polar types or by subjecting data from a substantial number of cases to statistical analysis. Let us assume the problem is whether bureaucratization adversely affects work satisfaction. One approach is to examine intensively two organizations, which are highly similar in many respects, but which differ sharply in degree of bureaucratization, and to ascertain whether these differences in bureaucratization, and variations in degree of bureaucratization within either organization, affect various aspects of work satisfaction. Another approach is to collect from a large number of organizations data on a few readily ascertainable manifestations of bureaucratization and some simple measures of work satisfaction, such as turnover rates, and determine the correlation coefficients between the former and the latter. The first approach is more similar to the case study, providing more intensive data, but data of lesser scope than does the quantitative study. Although the quantitative study provides more reliable evidence for generalizations, it usually cannot tell us whether the assumed causal nexus is indeed correct. The fact that several indications of bureaucratization are positively correlated with turnover does not demonstrate that bureaucratization reduces work satisfaction, or even that it raises turnover. For it may be that the causal direction is the opposite and that high turnover rates give rise to more bureaucratic procedures as a means of regulating the work of large numbers of inexperienced employees.

At first glance, it appears that case studies have several advantages over the comparative method. Case studies provide intensive information in depth about social processes; they permit greater flexibility in the choice of variables to be studied; they allow the researcher to generate and test new hypotheses in the course of his study; and they yield data on the sequence of events from which the direction of casuality is more reliably inferred. Their serious weakness, however, is that the validity of inferences made from them is always subject to doubt. This problem is illustrated if we compare the conclusions of two case studies of a state employment agency. The first, written by the senior author of this book, argues that the use of statistical performance records decreases discrimination. The second case study, completed a decade later, finds just the opposite.

> Equitable treatment of clients was an important latent function of statistical records of performance in Department X. Interviewers eliminated personal considerations from their operations because this evaluation system focused their interest on maximizing placements. The greater the influence of production records on officials, the less were their operating decisions subject to ethnic bias. In Section A, the group most oriented toward productivity, the referral chances of Negroes were better than in Section B, where productivity was less emphasized; and there are indications that they were lowest in Section C, where placements counted least in the rating. Moreover, there was a direct relationship between the individual's concern with productivity, as indicated by competitive hoarding of jobs, and the extent to which he selected Negroes for referrals.[4]

[4] Peter M. Blau, *The Dynamics of Bureaucracy*, 2nd ed. (Chicago: University of Chicago Press, 1963), p. 94.

The pressures to make placements deriving from the personal evaluation and budgetary systems (reflected on the local level in detailed interviewer statistical records of operations) were quite likely to cause discriminatory referrals. . . . Referral of nonwhite clients to an employer who does not want them can cause complete halt of all future placement operations with this employer. If placements are hard to come by (i.e., if conditions are such that few applicants are being hired), and the industry is one in which many employers desire discriminatory referrals, then this pressure is likely to cause "gentlemen's agreements" where the agency staff do not refer nonwhite clients to such employers, and do not report these discriminatory requests to the Anti-discrimination commission as obliged under the law. Placements are important to interviewers, but employers control placements by hiring or rejecting referred applicants. Hence, interviewers follow predominant employer desires rather than anti-discrimination procedures in order to maximize statistical placement records.[5]

Some reconciliation of these two accounts is possible, of course. The first is primarily concerned with prejudice on the part of the interviewers in employment agencies. In the second description the emphasis is upon discriminatory behavior that is the result of prejudice on the part of employers. It might be said that statistical records of performance render employment interviewers more impersonal in doing their jobs—less likely to let their own prejudices influence their own decisions, but even more likely to discriminate against blacks in response to pressures from employers who do not want to hire them. Nonetheless, the difference between the two interpretations indicates how easily generalizations derived from case studies can be misleading.

A case study may yield inferences that do not hold for most organizations precisely because only one organization is being studied. Nothing guarantees that any one bureaucracy is in most respects similar to the huge population of

[5] Harry Cohen, *The Demonics of Bureaucracy* (Ames: State University of Iowa Press, 1965), pp. 187–188.

organizations about which generalizations are implicitly made. Just as a survey analyst would not attempt to predict the outcome of an election on the basis of a handful of interviews, a statement cannot be made about organizations generally from knowledge of only one or two. The survey analyst requires a large and carefully selected sample of respondents in order to be confident that his findings are representative of the whole population. In the same manner, a student of organizations needs information about a large number of bureaucracies in order to be confident that his results reflect general tendencies. Evidently, generalizations cannot be made on the basis of a single case—whether the generalizations are about people, organizations, or nation-states. It is possible to study one case at a time in order to accumulate knowledge, or experiments involving one subject (or a single case) can be repeated a number of times. But no matter what the procedure, the principle is still the same: meaningful generalizations can be established only after there exists information about a large number of cases of the phenomenon under study.

Some Findings of Comparative Organizational Research

Comparative studies of all organizations of a given type, or a representative sample of them, can demonstrate what the relationships between organizational characteristics are, and that is their great virtue. They can answer the questions the organizational theorist poses, and they consequently provide him with the material to refine his theory, notably if the answers are not entirely what he anticipated, as is often the case. For example, they can answer such questions as which ones of the various characteristics Weber considers typical of bureaucracies actually tend to occur together, or whether large organizations have proportionately larger administrative machineries than small ones and devote more of their personnel to administering the bureaucracy rather than to contributing directly to its objectives. To be sure, the theorist is ultimately interested in discovering general principles that apply to all organizations of any type, but comparative research can only establish the validity of generalizations for the organizations under investigation, not for substantially different types. It is impossible to obtain empirical data on all types of organizations; neither is it possible to collect data from a sample representative of all possible types, since we have no idea what the universe of all types of organizations is. Hence, research findings can never definitively establish the most basic theoretical generalizations. Nevertheless, our confidence in theoretical generalizations about the interdependence of organizational characteristics is greatly strengthened if they are corroborated by empirical findings from comparative research on a large number of organizations or, still better, from several such studies of different types of organizations. Let us illustrate such findings and their theoretical implications from recent comparative research on organizations.

Clusters of Organizational Characteristics

Weber's ideal-typical description of bureaucracy, discussed in Chapter 2, includes these elements: division of labor and specialization, a hierarchy of authority, an administrative staff, compensation that is related to one's position, continuity of operations and employment, and the use of contracts or agreements which specify in advance a person's obligations to the organization. Implicit in Weber's model is the notion that organizational rewards are based on performance. It could be argued that these attributes of bureaucracy are interdependent—that is, the presence of any one makes it more likely that any of the others will appear. For instance, because the division of labor increases the need for coordination, a hierarchy of authority is developed. Procedures and regulations are then required to insure consistent operations in all parts of an organization; it is the task of an administrative staff to formulate them. In any case, if it is true that these elements distinguish bureaucratic from less bureaucratic organizations, then in a large sample of organizations one ought to find positive correlations among these bureaucratic attributes.

Comparative studies of organizations have found that not all rational organizations include the characteristics of bureaucracy that Weber considers essential to efficient operations. Two comparative studies of entirely different kinds of organizations come, quite independently, to very similar conclusions. Stinchcombe contrasts the organization of work in the American construction and mass-production industries; Stanley Udy analyzes simple work organizations in 150 different nonindustrial societies.[6] Both studies examine most of the factors mentioned above, and both find that there apparently are two clusters of organizational attributes, one of which might be called "bureaucratic" and the other "rational." The "bureaucratic" characteristics include a hierarchy of authority of several levels, an administrative staff, continuity of operations, and compensation according to one's position. The cluster of "rational" attributes includes specialization of the work force, contractual obligations, and rewards based on performance. The characteristics within each cluster are interrelated, but none of the "bureaucratic" characteristics are positively related to any of the "rational" ones. (The two terms are in quotation marks because they refer merely to the characteristics in the two clusters.) In short, the fact that the work of a group of people is "rationally" organized has no bearing on whether or not the organization will assume a "bureaucratic" form.

Weber's ideal type seems to include two distinct sets of organizational attributes, which, as the empirical data indi-

[6] Arthur L. Stinchcombe, "Bureaucratic and Craft Administration of Production," *Administrative Science Quarterly*, 4 (1959), 168–187; and Stanley Udy, Jr., " 'Bureaucracy' and 'Rationality' in Weber's Theory," *American Sociological Review*, 24 (1959), 791–795.

cate, should be kept separate. If the systematic organization and coordination of the work of a group of people entails some specialization, one usually also finds that contracts or agreements stipulate the obligations of the various participants and that the rewards each receives are assumed to depend on the contribution his performance makes to the collective effort. Such a rational organization of collective effort may be found in simple organizations which do not operate continuously as well as in permanently established complex bureaucracies, which are usually characterized by a multilevel hierarchy of authority, a sizable administrative component (managers, staff specialists, and clerks), and rewards differentiated by official position. What conditions discourage the development of complex bureaucracies in an industry? Stinchcombe's comparison of construction and mass-production industries in this country provides a clue for answering this question. He suggests that seasonal fluctuation in construction makes it uneconomical to maintain permanent large bureaucracies, and the high skills of the craftsmen in production make rational operations possible without a permanent administrative machinery. Hence, small contractors and subcontractors, who hire and lay off craftsmen as needed, are mostly found in construction, whereas large bureaucratic factories predominate in mass production. The implication is that a bureaucratic organization can rationalize the work process without depending on a highly skilled labor force, therefore, effecting reductions in labor costs.

Although these research findings require revision of part of Weber's theoretical conception, they also provide indirect support for other parts of his theory. Not all characteristics of bureaucracies he subsumes under the ideal type are interdependent. Some are as often found in simple organizations as in complex bureaucracies. On the other hand, his generalization that large-scale continuous administrative tasks lead to the development of bureaucracies is supported by the finding that the organizations in an industry are less bureaucratic if seasonal fluctuations interfere with continuous operations. Moreover, the implication that the bureaucratic organizations in mass production permit rational operations at lower labor costs supports Weber's generalization that bureaucratization furthers efficiency.

Formal Structure and Decision-Making

Many theories of bureaucracy stress the importance of decision-making in large organizations. Yet the relationship of organizational characteristics to the way decisions are made has not been widely studied. Case studies and theoretical statements have suggested a number of hypotheses, however. Crozier's description of French bureaucracy, for example, indicates that the combination of multiple levels of hierarchy and highly centralized decision-making has dysfunctions: those who have authority to make decisions lack sufficient information, while those who have information lack authority.[7] It might be inferred that in general, as a result of the pressure to avoid such inefficiency, an increase in the number of hierarchial levels in an organization is accompanied by a tendency to decentralize decisions. French bureaucracies are exceptions to this pattern and are inefficient for this reason. Comparative research on 46 British organizations, mostly private firms, confirms this prediction, as does a study of 254 American government agencies.[8] The more levels there are in the hierarchy, the greater is the extent to which top management delegates decisions to subordinates. It has also been found that multiple levels of hierarchy together with decentralization are associated with the existence of formal rules and regulations

[7] Michel Crozier, *The Bureaucratic Phenomenon* (Chicago: University of Chicago Press, 1964), p. 108.

[8] D. S. Pugh, *et. al.*, "Dimensions of Organization Structure," *Administrative Science Quarterly*, 13 (1968), 65–105; and Marshall W. Meyer, "The Two Authority Structures of Bureaucratic Organization," *ibid.*, pp. 211–228.

which state organizational goals and set criteria for evaluating employees' performance. The rules function to guide decisions made by different people on a decentralized basis and insure that the decisions will be consistent with one another. It could be said that these rules and regulations serve as a substitute for directives from centralized authority.

Centralization of decision-making authority in the hands of top management tends to occur as the number of major subdivisions—divisions, departments, or sections—in an organization increases. Theories of administration, anticipating this finding, have noted that as the number of managers who head subdivisions and report to top management grows larger, the likelihood that any given decision will affect more than one of them increases. In a retail store, for example, if there is only one manager in charge of hard goods (who reports to the president), he can make all decisions that affect the selling of hard goods as long as they have no impact on soft-goods departments. If, however, there are two hard-goods managers, neither of them has authority to make decisions that affect all hard-goods departments. Such decisions must be made by the head of the store. Furthermore, the presence of two hard-goods managers means that there will be at least occasional disagreements between them. From time to time, their superior will have to resolve these disagreements, again contributing to the centralization of decision-making.

The number of hierarchical levels expresses vertical differentiation in an organization, and the number of major subdivisions is one indication of horizontal differentiation. In these terms, vertical differentiation promotes decentralization, whereas horizontal differentiation fosters centralization. But both dimensions of differentiation depend on an organization's size. Large organizations have more hierarchical levels and more horizontal subdivisions than small ones. When size is controlled, however, one can see that the two dimensions of differentiation are inversely related. For organizations of a given size, the larger the number of levels, the smaller is the number of subdivisions. Many major subdivisions entail a wide span of control and hence a heavy administrative burden for top management. Vertical differentiation into multilevel hierarchies, because it decreases the number of subdivisions, reduces the top executives' load of administrative responsibilities. Some organizations tend to develop squat pyramids, and others tall ones, and the shape of the organization's pyramid is associated with the distribution of responsibilities in it. Centralized decision-making is characteristic of squat hierarchies, whereas decentralization of responsibilities tends to prevail in tall structures with multiple hierarchical levels.

Size and Proportion of Administrative Personnel

It has been widely believed that the growth of organizations gives rise to the cancerous growth of their administrative machineries. The popular conception of the overbureaucratization of large organizations implies this, and so does Parkinson's Law. The larger an organization, according to this reasoning, the larger is the share of its total personnel required to administer it and keep it going, and the smaller is, therefore, the proportion of its employees who perform the organization's basic function, be it manufacturing cars in a factory or caring for the sick in a hospital. Indeed, the assumption is not implausible that large organizations have disproportionately large administrative overheads, which impede their efficiency. We know that production firms today tend to be larger than they were at the beginning of the century and that the relative size of their administrative staffs has exhibited a similar increase during this period, which makes the inference plausible that their larger size accounts for their expanded administrative overhead. We also know that large organizations have a more complex structure than small ones, and it is reasonable to assume that the greater complexity of large organizations increases the need for administrative personnel. Plausible as these inferences are, however, comparative research reveals them to be false.

The larger an organization is, the smaller is the proportionate size of its administrative component. This conclusion, which flatly contradicts the popular myth of the excessive administrative overhead of large bureaucracies, is supported by numerous comparative studies of various types of organizations, using different measures of administrative component.[9] Whether business firms, hospitals, school districts, universities, or government agencies are examined, there is an inverse relationship between an organization's size and the proportion of its administrative personnel. If the administrative ratio in production firms today tends to be higher than it was at the beginning of the century, this is probably because they are more complex today, not because they are larger. For research indicates that a complex structure increases the ratio of administrative personnel in an organization. But despite the fact that large organizations are more complex than small ones and complexity raises the administrative ratio, this ratio generally declines with increasing size, because the economies in administrative personnel that large size makes possible tend to outweigh the extra administrative personnel that the complexity of large organizations requires.

Caveat

Modern organizations are complex structures composed of many interdependent elements. A theory of organizations

---

[9] See, for example, Seymour Melman, "The Rise of Administrative Overhead in the Manufacturing Industries of the United States, 1899–1947," *Oxford Economic Papers*, 3 (1951), 61–112; Theodore R. Anderson and Seymour Warkov, "Organizational Size and Functional Complexity," *American Sociological Review*, 26 (1961), 23–28; Amos H. Hawley, *et al.*, "Population Size and Administration in Institutions of Higher Education," *American Sociological Review*, 30 (1965), 252–255; Bernard P. Indik, "The Relationship Between Organization Size and Supervision Ratio," *Administrative Science Quarterly*, 9 (1964), 301–312; and Peter M. Blau and Richard A. Schoenherr, *The Structure of Organizations* (New York: Basic Books, 1971), Chap. 4.

that can explain why they have various characteristics requires both a knowledge of the relationships among organizational characteristics and an understanding of the social processes that produce these connections. Only the systematic comparison of large numbers of organizations can ascertain the complex interrelations that characterize their formal structure. But comparative quantitative studies lack the intensive information on internal processes needed to elucidate these connections. Case studies of organizations are best suited to provide these data, and they are also best suited to investigate in depth deviant cases to determine what accounts for the exception to the prevailing tendency. Until recently, virtually all research on organizations consisted of case studies, and these could not answer many of the questions of interest to the organizational theorist. The last decade has witnessed a growing interest in comparative organizational research, which is beginning to provide important empirical information heretofore unavailable. However, the significant contribution comparative research can make to organizational theory entails the danger that the value of case studies be entirely overlooked. This would be unfortunate, because comparative and case studies of organizations complement each other, and it is the combination of knowledge derived from both that promises to make the greatest contribution to the advancement of social science.

6

Bureaucracy and Social Change

If discipline does not suffice for effective bureaucratic operation, flexibility also being necessary, it follows that rigidity is disadvantageous for the organization. Whereas this principle has been stressed throughout the preceding discussion, we have not yet examined carefully the sociopsychological processes involved. Why do some members of large organizations resist any change in procedures while others accept innovations with ease? What are the organizational conditions in bureaucracies that give rise to these opposite tendencies?

This question of internal change is distinct from, though not unrelated to, the problem of external change, that is, bureaucracy's role in changing the society of which it is a part. Bureaucratization has been held to be a revolutionary force, on the one hand, and a potent instrument of reaction that makes it virtually impossible to alter the existing institutional structure, on the other. Again, there appear to be contradictory strains that require exploration.

Who Are the Ritualists?

"The clerks of departments find themselves sooner or later in the condition of a wheel screwed on to a machine; the only variation of their lot is to be more or less oiled." In these words, Balzac describes the lot of the bureaucrat in the novel *The Civil Service*. Students of administration similarly have often called attention to the ritualistic concern with the minutiae of routine and the resulting inefficiency that one often encounters in bureaucracies. An excerpt from a study of the civil service in France illustrates these conditions:

Every large-scale organization controlled from a single center sooner or later finds it advisable to elaborate systematic routine procedures in the interest of fiscal regularity and operational consistency. Private business corporations are no more immune to this process than are government departments. Nor do routine procedures necessarily slow up staff decisions. On the contrary, if they are properly adapted to the daily problems of the enterprise, they expedite action.

An organization conforming closely to the hierarchical principle, however, faces the constant danger that these routine operations will become sterilizing ends in themselves rather than effective means to desirable ends. When this happens the usual result is an entanglement of "red tape," or as the French are wont to call it, *La paperasserie, mere* routine thereby becoming *bad* routine. Formal instructions issued at the center overwhelm those who have to handle out on the circumference concrete situations unforeseen in their variety. Almost inevitably an adequate delegation of discretion to subordinate officials is missing in such a system and the field agent stationed on the administrative firing line stands helpless before demands for prompt decision and immediate action. The fact that every case must be "referred" somewhere means a postponement of any decision about it, the more circuitous the course of reference, the greater the delay. . . .

Mr. Ford Madox Ford relates his adventures in trying to

trace a postal money order gone astray. When this occurs, the usual course is to take the matter up through official channels, give the postman a big tip, or put the case into the hands of "an adviser of public companies." On this occasion, however, Mr. Ford decided to go directly to the *Direction de la Seine des P. T. T.* on the Boulevard Montparnasse. At two o'clock he was ushered into the Director's office by a smiling char-woman. After a half hour the Director returned from lunch and scrutinized the documents with great care. Following further consultation with an official in a blue uniform, the Director announced that Ford should betake himself to the "Chief Sub-office for the Recovery of Money Orders" on the other side of Paris. There he was directed to Room V on the sixth floor. While he conversed with an attractive young woman for an hour about face powders and the like, her chief examined the papers and asked questions about Ford's war record and family, finally instructing him to return to the Boulevard Montparnasse, this time to Room XVI on the third floor. From there he was sent back to Room XI in the Chief Sub-office; thence to Room IV, Boulevard Montparnasse; next to Room III, Chief Suboffice; and finally to the "open ses-ame"–Room XIII, on Montparnasse. Although assured there that he would receive his money by the first delivery the following day, it actually arrived seven weeks later, only after a generous tip had been showered upon the postman.[1]

Inefficiency of this sort occurs when the members of an organization become so preoccupied with meticulous appli-cation of detailed rules that they lose sight of the very purpose of their action. Certain conditions in bureaucratic structures encourage the development of this ritualistic orientation, as Merton notes:

Discipline can be effective only if the ideal patterns are but-tressed by strong sentiments which entail devotion to one's

---

[1] Walter R. Sharp, *The French Civil Service* (New York: Macmillan, 1931), pp. 446–450, by permission of the Macmillan Company. Re-printed in Robert K. Merton, Ailsa P. Gray, Barbara Hockey, and Hanan C. Selvin (eds.), *Reader in Bureaucracy* (Glencoe, Ill.: Free Press, 1952), pp. 407–409.

duties, a keen sense of the limitation of one's authority and competence, and methodical performance of routine activities. The efficacy of social structure depends ultimately upon infusing group participants with appropriate attitudes and sentiments. . . . These sentiments are often more intense than is technically necessary. There is a margin of safety, so to speak, in the pressure exerted by these sentiments upon the bureaucrat to conform to his patterned obligations, in much the same sense that added allowances (precautionary overestimations) are made by the engineer in designing the supports for a bridge. But this very emphasis leads to a transference of the sentiments from the *aims* of the organization onto the particular details of behavior required by the rules. Adherence to the rules, originally conceived as a means, becomes transformed into an end-in-itself; there occurs the familiar process of *displacement of goals* whereby "an instrumental value becomes a terminal value." Discipline, readily interpreted as conformance with regulations, whatever the situation, is seen not as a measure designed for specific purposes but becomes an immediate value in the life-organization of the bureaucrat.[2]

The prevention of arbitrary decisions requires that a high respect for disciplined performance of duties be fostered among the members of a bureaucracy. This emphasis sometimes becomes overpowering, with the result that punctilious adherence to formalized procedures is elevated into the primary objective of bureaucratic activities and displaces their original objectives in the thinking of officials. Compelled by this orientation to find the right rule before making the least commitment, a bureaucrat will refuse to take any action if there is no clearcut precedent or if there is the slightest doubt about whether it is entirely within his official sphere of jurisdiction. The well-known phenomenon of "passing the buck" and other practices that obstruct operations are often expressions of this tendency. In one case, an official in the employment agency previously mentioned postponed deciding on the color of a new set of

[2] Robert K. Merton, *Social Theory and Social Structure*, 3rd ed. (New York: Free Press, 1968), pp. 252–253. By permission.

index cards until he could determine what color they were "supposed" to have, completely ignoring that the only purpose of assigning a color to them was to distinguish them from other sets of cards. Officials who find their security in strict adherence to familiar routines, moreover, strongly resist changes in the organization and are incapacitated by new problems that confront them. Rigidities are dysfunctional for operating efficiency even under stable conditions and particularly when emergent problems call for a reorganization of working procedures.

Ritualistic displacement of goals, however, is not characteristic of all members of bureaucratic organizations. Many of them, far from deriving satisfaction from constantly following the same routine, find doing so extremely boring. They often express a desire for more variety in their work and for changes that would relieve its monotony. Since even complex tasks become less interesting once they are fully mastered, many employees welcome frequent changes in procedures because these create new problems which recurrently make their work challenging. As one civil servant in the federal agency discussed in Chapter 3 put it: "Lots of us gripe about the fact that they change things all the time. But if I should be completely honest with you, although I also gripe about having to keep on learning new things, I really like it. That's what keeps the job interesting."

Some officials rigidly oppose innovations in the organization, while others favor them. What are the structural constraints in bureaucracies that account for these differences? One of them is the nature of the incentive system. When strict conformity with specific operating rules is the basis for evaluation, employees are motivated, as a way of adapting to this situation, to think of bureaucratic procedures as if they were a sacred ritual, and strong resistance to change in these procedures must be expected. When employees, on the other hand, are evaluated in terms of the results accomplished in their operations, they are encouraged to exercise ingenuity and employ diverse methods in the interest of maximizing specified accomplishments. But even in the situation where the evaluation system itself does not foster ritualism, other conditions in the bureaucratic structure may do so.

An analysis of instances of extreme rigidity in hierarchical organizations reveals that they are usually associated with fear of superiors. For example, a group of officials was once reprimanded by a high administrative official for having made an incorrect decision in one of its cases. Thereupon, they applied the rules literally in similar cases and refrained from exercising any discretion even when it was clearly called for; afraid of further reprimand, they attempted to protect themselves against this danger with overconformity. Bureaucratic superiors cannot generally censure a subordinate for following official regulations exactly, regardless of how inefficient or ridiculous such action may be in a particular case. Indeed, prisoners sometimes resort to rigid overconformity as a deliberate form of sabotage. The typical case is inadvertent, however: feelings of dependency on superiors and anxiety over their reactions engender ritualistic tendencies.

Rigid adherence to the established routine is a defense mechanism against feelings of insecurity. In the study of the federal agency, the attitudes of a group of officials toward changes in regulations, which occurred frequently, were ascertained and related to their competence as investigators. Not one of the more competent half of this group, but most of the less competent half, voiced objections to these recurrent innovations. From a purely rational standpoint, the opposite finding might have been expected: the agent most familiar with existing regulations and most adept in applying them presumably should have been most disturbed when they were superseded by new ones. This reasoning, however, fails to take into consideration the emotional factors that influence conduct. The anxieties generated by the experience that one's knowledge is not always adequate for one's tasks can be calmed by making a ritual of conformity with those procedures with which one has become familiar. Changes in procedures constitute a threat to this method of coping with anxieties and, consequently, must be strenuously resisted. Only in the absence of predominant feelings of insecurity can the desire to escape monotony emerge as a motivating force. Officials who feel secure in their ability to handle their responsibilities and do not continually worry about the reactions of superiors conceive of new problems as stimulating challenges and welcome frequent changes which prevent their jobs from becoming monotonous.[3]

Bureaucracy as Instrument of Innovation

In the large and complex societies of today, the implementation of new social policies requires bureaucratic machinery. Consider inventions, which are sometimes viewed as spontaneous sources of social change. But take, for example, the case of the atomic bomb. To be sure, had Enrico Fermi and other scientists not had some brilliant ideas, there would be no atomic bomb, but these ideas alone did not bring it into existence. A complicated bureaucratic organization had to be set up both to produce atomic bombs and to furnish scientists with laboratories where they could work together on improvements and new developments. Not that all social change in modern society is bureaucratically instituted. New customs constantly arise without the intervention of bureaucracies. But the deliberate introduction of a social innovation on a large scale, whether it involves the production of a new weapon or the enforcement of a new law, depends on bureaucratic methods of administration.

Trade unions illustrate this point and some of its implications. For workers to realize their collective goal of improving their standard of living, they organized. To establish a

[3] This situation probably also holds for teachers and other professions.

strong labor union against the opposition of employers was, and still is, a very difficult task. It could not have been accomplished unless many workers, at least temporarily, had set aside their economic interests, often sacrificing their jobs and sometimes their very lives, because they were idealists whose primary objective was the creation of an effective labor organization. The need for such idealism in the establishment of trade unions was pointed out a century ago by Karl Marx, the man who is often assumed to interpret social conduct as determined primarily by economic interests and not by ideas. He wrote:

> If the first aim of the general resistance was merely the maintenance of wages, combinations [of workers], at first isolated, constitute themselves into groups as the capitalists in their turn unite in the idea of repression, and in the face of always united capital, the maintenance of the association [union] becomes more necessary to them than that of wages. This is so true that the English economists are amazed to see the workers sacrifice a good part of their wages in favor of associations, which in the eyes of the economists, are established solely in favor of wages.[4]

Without using the term, Marx described in this passage the process of displacement of goals from high wages to maintenance of the organization. Observing the early struggles of the labor movement, he assumed this process to be highly beneficial for it. The findings of more recent studies of trade unions suggest that he was too optimistic, in this respect as in many others. Displacement of goals frequently results in a preoccupation with keeping the bureaucratic apparatus going at the expense of its basic objectives.

Robert Michels' famous study of labor unions and democratic parties in Germany at the beginning of the present century is concerned with this problem. Even a socialist

[4] Karl Marx, *The Poverty of Philosophy* (New York: International Publishers, 1963), p. 145; quoted in Reinhard Bendix and Seymour M. Lipset, *Class, Status and Power*, 2nd ed. (New York: Free Press, 1966), p. 9.

party or a progressive union, regardless of how egalitarian its principles, must establish a hierarchical bureaucracy to put its reform program into effect. (The issues raised by this so-called "iron law of oligarchy" will be discussed in the last chapter.) The major interest of party or union officials is to strengthen the organization, not only because their jobs depend on its survival, but also because a powerful machine is needed in the fight for the intended reforms. In this respect, the self-interest of the leadership and the collective interest of the membership coincide. Officials, consequently, are willing to make great sacrifices for the sake of fortifying the organization. To attract more members, they will abandon unpopular points of the program. To prevent the possibility of a crushing defeat, they will refrain from calling a strike to enforce union demands. "Thus, from a means, organization becomes an end."[5] Step by step, the original objectives are surrendered in the interest of increased organizational strength. The resulting organization may be extremely strong, but it is no longer an instrument for effecting the radical changes initially planned. What was once a socialist party (or a radical union) has turned into a rather conservative one. The inevitable fate of all radical movements, according to Michels, is to grow conservative in the course of becoming organized.

This conclusion has important implications that extend far beyond the question of the future of socialism. The radical ideas of the Reformation spread more or less spontaneously without the aid of a bureaucratic apparatus, producing profound changes in the institutional structure of European society. Michels suggested that this cannot happen in today's bureaucratized societies. For new ideas to find expression in institutional change, they must be bureaucratically implemented. In the process of creating an effective bureaucratic apparatus, radical new ideas are always

[5] Robert Michels, *Political Parties* (Glencoe, Ill.: Free Press, 1949), p. 373.

renounced in favor of more conservative ones. This is the dilemma of radical movements; they need bureaucracy, yet are undermined by it. Michels implies that people cannot possibly control their common destiny by instituting desirable social reforms. For unless they establish a bureaucratic organization for this purpose, they will not be successful in realizing their new ideals, and if they do, they will abandon them. There is reason to assume, however, that this impasse is not entirely insurmountable. Although Michels analyzed a doubtlessly prevalent feature of organizational life, he ignored another trend that points in the opposite direction.

An examination of unions and parties that began with a very radical program reveals, indeed, that most of those that survived replaced their earlier radical goals with more moderate ones and greater concern with administrative matters in the course of establishing an effective organization. But a look at unions that initially had more limited plans for change discloses different tendencies. The American labor movement provides a good illustration. After the decline eighty years ago of the Knights of Labor, who had advocated a radical political program, most unions confined their efforts to the pursuit of two objectives: establishing the right of collective bargaining and raising wages. To be sure, concern with building a strong union sometimes pushed these two goals into the background, as jurisdictional strikes indicate, and some union leaders became increasingly conservative.[6] The main development, however, was not the one stressed by Michels: unions did not relinquish their original objectives. Quite the contrary, they achieved them in large part and strove for new, further-reaching reforms. Thus, the right of collective bargaining supplied a basis for the fight for workers' pensions, a social innovation far surpassing the aspirations of union members a

[6] See Alvin W. Gouldner, "Attitudes of 'Progressive' Trade-Union Leaders," *American Journal of Sociology*, 52 (1947), 389–392.

few decades ago. This process, the reverse of displacement of goals, can be called "succession of goals"; as earlier objectives are attained, they become stepping stones for new ones.

The succession of goals, of course, is not primarily the result of the superior idealism of American as compared with German labor leaders, but the consequence of structural constraints in the organization. Once a union has achieved its major objectives, the enthusiasm of its members tends to wane. Many withdraw their support, financially and otherwise, and thereby threaten the persistence of the organization. The very fact that union officials are interested in maintaining their jobs and power constrains them to seek new ways of stimulating membership support. An effective method for recreating vigorous interest in union affairs is to establish new objectives for which workers are willing to fight. Hence, new goals often emerge in organizations as old ones have been reached. This is the case not only in unions but also in other organizations marked by bureaucracy's stamp.[7]

What determines whether displacement of goals or succession of goals predominates in an organization? This crucial question can be only partially answered. When the original objectives of a social movement arouse intense hostility and violent attacks, the insecurity of its members and their preoccupation with creating an organization and preserving it are likely to constrain them to compromise their ideals in order to avoid annihilation. When the community permits an organization, if only by default, to become established and attain at least some of its first objectives in a relatively short period, it will probably find new fields to conquer in the course of its development. How radical can social movements be without provoking

[7] See Peter M. Blau, *The Dynamics of Bureaucracy*, 2nd ed. (Chicago: University of Chicago Press, 1963), pp. 241–244; and David L. Sills, *The Volunteers* (New York: Free Press, 1957), pp. 254–264.

hostilities that destroy them? How long is the period of grace before the struggle is given up as hopeless and the initial objectives are abandoned to maintain the organization? We do not yet know the answers to these questions, although some recent research provides suggestive leads to the study of interconnections between organizational factors and social change.

Conservative Pressures in Three Social Contexts

A brief review of empirical investigations of reform programs and their fate indicates the complex relationship between bureaucratic structures and changes in social policies. Whereas all three studies to be reviewed found strains toward conservativism, the social forces responsible for them were quite different.

Philip Selznick's study of the Tennessee Valley Authority (TVA) shows that the grass-roots policy adopted by this New Deal agency had unanticipated consequences that brought about fundamental changes in its progressive program.[8] The TVA was established during the depression of the 1930s by the federal government to supply inexpensive electricity to predominantly rural areas. The principle of grass-roots democracy emphasizes that the central government should not simply impose its authority upon the people in a region, but should give them a voice in the management of the federal agencies that affect their lives. Since all people in the Tennessee Valley could not directly participate in administrative decisions, this principle was implemented in actual practice by appointing representatives of powerful local institutions, notably the land-grant colleges, to positions on the policy-making body of the TVA. Many of these influential persons and organizations

[8] Philip Selznick, *TVA and the Grass Roots* (Berkeley and Los Angeles: University of California Press, 1949).

had been strongly opposed to the TVA, and their opposition might well have put serious obstacles in its way. The cooptation of representatives of these powerful conservative groups by the TVA, that is, their absorption into its leadership structure, averted this threat. The grass-roots method, as it was interpreted, constituted a mechanism that permitted a New Deal agency to function in a region dominated by conservative forces.

The initial commitment to work through locally established institutions had unforeseen effects that, paradoxically, contradicted the democratic spirit of the grass-roots doctrine that had been the reason for making the commitment. As men with conservative views who represented vested interests and not the majority of people in the area were appointed to its board of directors, TVA's policies became increasingly conservative and removed from New Deal principles. Thus, the TVA discriminated against blacks; it came into conflict with other New Deal agencies, such as the Farm Security Administration; and various policies that had been designed to protect the public interest against special private interests were reversed. The last point is exemplified by the changes that occurred in the purchase of land for reservoirs. Building a reservoir improves the soil around it. To permit the public, whose funds paid for the reservoir, to benefit from this increment in land value, the TVA established the policy that the purchase of land for each reservoir include a surrounding protective strip 300 to 1,000 feet wide. Many landowners, anxious to reap these benefits themselves, were opposed to this program of public ownership. Since their interest was represented on TVA's board, their pressure was successful. In 1942, the policy was reversed, the board of directors deciding "to limit the purchase of land for reservoir purposes to the minimum appropriate for the particular project,"[9] which usually did not include any protective strip.

[9] *Ibid.*, p. 204.

Selznick does not deny that the TVA produced profound changes in the Tennessee Valley and greatly contributed to the welfare of its economically deprived people. But he shows that these changes were not so far-reaching and not so unequivocally in the interest of the larger population in the area as had been originally planned. In the course of its development, the bureaucracy became more conservative.

S. M. Lipset, in his study of a socialist government in a Canadian province, also observes that the bureaucratic implementation of a progressive program occasioned its modification.[10] When the CCF (Cooperative Commonwealth Federation) came into power in Saskatchewan in 1944 and its members took over all cabinet posts, they retained the former administrators of government bureaucracies as their deputies. Although it was known that most of the high government officials were middle-class persons not at all sympathetic to the socialist program of the CCF, the leaders held that they needed these administrative experts to operate the bureaucratic machinery in the various governmental departments. Moreover, ministers assumed that they would determine policy and that their deputies would only carry it out. In the process of being administered by conservative bureaucrats, however, socialist policies were often basically altered. Here are a few illustrations from Lipset's book:

> A number of civil servants were able to convince their ministers that certain changes were not administratively feasible or that they would incur too much opposition. Some deputy ministers exchanged information with other deputies on their technique of controlling their ministers. . . . Some key officials boasted of "running my department completely," and of "stopping harebrained radical schemes."

> One cabinet minister, who has since discharged a large part of his field staff, found as a result of complaints from local mem-

[10] S. M. Lipset, *Agrarian Socialism* (Berkeley and Los Angeles: University of California Press, 1950), pp. 255–275. By permission.

bers of the C.C.F. that members of his staff continued to grant leases and farming privileges to well-to-do persons who had secured them under previous governments, though it was now government policy to give them to poorer farmers and land-less veterans.

One cabinet minister decided that certain government work that had previously been contracted out to private concerns should be done by government employees whenever possible. His deputy minister, however, continued sending the work out to private concerns.[11]

An important similarity marks the findings of Lipset and Selznick, but there is also a difference that, though less obvious, is no less important. If we focus our attention upon the political program, we notice the similarity. In both instances, a progressive program was modified in the course of being implemented by bureaucratic methods. If we focus our attention upon the bureaucratic organization, on the other hand, we can see that it played quite a different role in the two cases. In Saskatchewan, bureaucracies obstructed plans for reform that had originated elsewhere, whereas in Tennessee, external forces obstructed, partly through infiltration, the bureaucracy's original plans for reform. The fact that government policy was modified in a conservative direction in both cases reveals the power of conservative forces in Canadian and American society. In one case, however, conservative pressure was exercised *by* bureaucracies, and its success indicates their strength; in the other case, conservative pressures were exercised *upon* the bureaucracy, and their success indicates its weakness.

It should be noted that neither of these two studies suggests that the bureaucratic structure itself generated the conservative trend. Selznick shows that in the case of the TVA it originated outside the bureaucracy, and Lipset stresses that in Saskatchewan it was due to the conservative orientation of the particular officials and not to inherent

[11] *Ibid.*, pp. 263, 265, 266–267.

tendencies in the bureaucratic form of organization. More-over, many parts of the progressive programs of the TVA and the CCF were actually realized.

A third case, however, does suggest that conditions of bureaucracy itself can inhibit social change and contribute to the defeat of a reform program. The war on poverty declared by President Lyndon B. Johnson in 1964 was in-tended not only to provide economic aid but also to stimu-late community participation of the poor and enhance their political influence. The lack of success of this program is analyzed in an article by Edgar and Jean Cahn. Poverty, they note, reflects a state of mind as much as a state of need. A sense of powerlessness, of inability to control one's environment, is often the psychological concomitant of economic privation, and, according to the Cahns, the pov-erty program succeeded only in exacerbating these feelings. Three characteristics of the program were responsible. First the "war" was fought by professionals on behalf of the citizenry with the aim of rendering service in accordance with the professionals' own judgments. Second, once objec-tives and strategies were determined, it became obligatory to adhere to the plan and the procedures established. Third, the program was to utilize all the resources available in the community, including the support of the incumbent politi-cal administration and of charitable and educational insti-tutions.

The Cahns point out that these characteristics of the war on poverty help undermine the self-confidence of the poor. When the task is defined as providing professional services, a "donor-donee" relationship is established.

All too easily such relationships become a means of per-petuating dependency rather than terminating it. A service program fills a need, but experts, not recipients, designate the need to be filled and establish the criteria for eligibility for aid. Typically, there is no effective means of challenging the basic criteria or for obtaining review of particular decisions applying these criteria. The pattern of aid is one of a donee's unquestioning acceptance, of an expert's dictation of what is "good for the client," and of an administrator's unchecked and unreviewable authority to terminate assistance. That power defines a status of subserviency and evokes fear, resentment and resignation on the part of the donee.[12]

A strategy that meticulously defines procedures and objectives has similar effects. It means centralized planning without participation of the poor. Effort is devoted toward achieving visible success, and little attention is directed toward the special needs of neighborhoods and groups of people. A reluctance to experiment or innovate becomes manifest, for a wartime strategy includes plans for the inevitable victory. Finally, cooperation with established community institutions renders opposition to them impossible and domination of the poverty program by them probable.

What was at issue in the war on poverty was not merely to bring about a social change, improvement in the conditions of the poor, but to do so by new democratic methods that would permit the poor to participate in the decisions regarding how their conditions should be improved. It was with respect to the latter objective of stimulating democratic participation that the poverty program failed, according to the Cahns and other critics. There is an important parallel with Michels' analysis of labor unions here. The bureaucratic organizations designed to carry out the poverty program undermined the poor's ability to exercise influence over this program, though strengthening this ability was one of the program's objectives. Similarly, the bureaucratization of unions undermines the ability of the rank and file to exercise influence over their unions, even if it helps workers to achieve other economic objectives. Bureaucracies are hierarchical structures in which ultimate authority rests at the apex, and while some of it is decentral-

---

[12] Edgar S. and Jean C. Cahn, "The War on Poverty," *Yale Law Journal*, 73 (1964), 1321–1322.

ized to lower levels, authority in bureaucracies is not allocated to the people they serve. Although bureaucracies are not necessarily resistant to social change and can actually be instruments of innovation, they are not suited to bring about changes involving greater democratic participation. For the bureaucratic form of organization is antithetical to the democratic form, a point which will be clarified in the final chapter.

7

The Transformation of Bureaucracy

Modern organizations differ markedly from their counterparts of as little as a few decades ago. Certain changes are all too obvious. Organizations are larger, more complex, and they rely more on advanced technologies than ever before. Other changes have been more subtle; some, perhaps, have passed unnoticed. The concern for efficiency has probably become more intense, not because of any increase in human avarice but because of new administrative techniques allowing managers to link inputs to outputs, costs to benefits. The forms of authority once thought characteristic of all organizations—authority based on commands and strict subordination—have greatly diminished in importance. Also, attitudes that people bring to their jobs are not what they used to be. These observations are not based on systematic empirical data. Rather, they stem from impressions stimulated by a number of sources. But what impressionistic evidence we have is so consistent that it suggests a transformation of bureaucracy, a movement away from traditional forms of organizations and toward bureaucracies that are more amorphous and less directive than they once were, organizations that satisfy their members' interests while operating at a high level of efficiency.

We should not be surprised to find that organizations are changing at a rapid clip; so is everything else. Yet few people stop to think of what most organizations were like during the last half of the nineteenth century. The efficient bureaucracies Weber described when he wrote his classic essay were more the exception than the rule then. Intensive division of labor, multilevel hierarchies, and the use of trained experts were only beginning to become common in public administration. In industry, a similar situation prevailed. The scientific management movement which dates from 1911 counseled employers to specify workers' duties and train them in their jobs. Today this is done as a matter of course. But at the turn of the century the development of efficient administrative organizations was in its first stages in many places, and in factories it was common practice to let a worker figure out what to do and how to do it—subject to often arbitrary and capricious supervision. Organizations have changed so much since 1900 that there is no reason to consider their present forms fixed or stagnant. In this chapter we examine the transformation of bureaucracy as it continues in the second half of this century. In particular, we are concerned with the question of efficiency, the effects of modern technology, and the significance of new impersonal mechanisms of control.

Questions of Efficiency

Weber's analysis emphasizes that the bureaucratic form of organization promotes administrative efficiency. "Precision, speed, unambiguity . . ., reduction of friction and of material and personal costs—these are raised to the optimum point in the strictly bureaucratic administration."[1] We essentially accept this view, though it should be pointed out that many critics take exception to it. Bureaucracy is often seen as symbolizing red tape, inefficiency, and arbitrary domination of clients by insensitive officials. Here we wish to explore whether recent changes in administrative practice contribute to or alleviate whatever inefficiencies develop in bureaucratic structures.

Problems

Several difficulties with this type of inquiry should be noted at the outset, however. No one can determine if bureaucracy is "efficient" or "inefficient." To say that bureaucracy is efficient (or inefficient) is an existential statement that cannot be confirmed or disconfirmed empirically; it is largely a matter of defining the terms involved. Scientists can most easily deal with statements that take the form "the more of X, the more of Y." One such proposition might be that *increasing* bureaucratization contributes to efficiency. But even this turns out to be untestable because bureaucratization is a complex process which involves contradictory tendencies. As noted in Chapter 5, the characteristics Weber thought most typical of bureaucracy do not necessarily appear together in organizations. It would be most sensible to separate the different characteristics—advanced division of labor, multilevel hierarchy, proliferation of rules and regulations, and so forth—and examine whether and how much each contributes to efficiency. Moreover, the notion of efficiency is itself quite elusive. The physical scientist thinks of a machine's efficiency as its ratio of output to input. Managers of organizations would also like to compute such ratios, but more often than not,

[1] Max Weber, "Bureaucracy," in H. H. Gerth and C. Wright Mills (eds.), *From Max Weber: Essays in Sociology* (New York: Oxford University Press, 1958), p. 214.

inputs, outputs, or both cannot be precisely measured. Techniques for evaluating organizational efficiency have been devised, but, as we shall see, they may not be wholly satisfactory.

Another problem is the difference between the intended effects of a formally designed institution and its actual effects. Bureaucratic organizations may well have been designed to maximize efficiency, but certain emergent practices within them may impede effective operations. Displacement of goals, to use Merton's term,[2] occurs when organizational means designed to promote efficiency become ends in themselves and are applied blindly to every case regardless of their consequences. When bureaucrats are taught to comply rigidly with the rules to insure uniformity and prevent favoritism, a trained incapacity results. Officials overconform and become insensitive to situations where exceptions should be granted and rules should be applied with discretion because of urgent need, or if only to expedite matters. Goal displacement is also rooted in another mechanism designed to promote efficiency. Many workers expect lifelong careers in a single organization and can be dismissed only for cause, and as long as they conform to all the rules there is no cause which might jeopardize their jobs or salary increases based on seniority.

A further question about organizational efficiency is raised by some neoclassical economists who draw the distinction between bureaucratic and profit-centered management. Bureaucracy is seen as "the method applied in the conduct of administrative affairs the result of which has no cash value on the market,"[3] or as an "organization in which the major portion of . . . output is not directly or indirectly evaluated in any markets external to the organi-

---

[2] Robert K. Merton, "Bureaucratic Structure and Personality," *Social Theory and Social Structure,* 3rd ed. (New York: Free Press, 1968), pp. 249–260.

[3] Ludwig Von Mises, *Bureaucracy* (New Haven: Yale University Press, 1944), p. 47.

zation."[4] These statements do not mean that what bureaucracies do has no value, but they do assert that the value cannot be measured. For example, no one denies that public education has value, but it is difficult to attach a dollar value to it. Lacking external markets, it is argued, bureaucratic organizations cannot judge their own performance. Rigidities and inefficiencies set in, and they are rarely corrected until a crisis occurs. Furthermore, since no objective criteria exist that would aid in assessing the performance of workers, the effectiveness of individual bureaucrats cannot be evaluated. They are thus assured careers and automatic advancement without meaningful review. To use the technical term, those who argue that bureaucracy is inefficient compared to other forms of organization claim this is so because bureaucracies lack *feedback mechanisms*, whereas profit-oriented organizations have them.

The feedback of information about his own organization which is available to a manager of a business is in the form of a statement of profit (or loss) from operations. The neoclassical economists who are critical of bureaucracy implicitly assume that maximization of profit is the only objective of business firms and that a profit and loss statement provides all the information a manager needs. This view, we think, is inadequate and obscures important similarities among organizations. One factor common to all organizations is the presence of multiple and conflicting goals. A business may seek to maximize its profit, and this goal may have primacy over others. Nonetheless the organization must pay some attention to the personal interests of its members if only for the sake of long-term profits. When members' interests are not satisfied, it becomes difficult to recruit employees and elicit their cooperation. Another goal of most organizations is viability—maintenance and expansion of the enterprise. Again, what is done to maximize

---

[4] Anthony Downs, *Inside Bureaucracy* (Boston: Little, Brown, 1966), p. 25.

short-term gain may in the long run injure viability. For example, monopolistic practices to raise profits may lead to antimonopoly legislation that endangers the organizations, as actually happened in this country around the turn of the century.

All organizations, those of the bureaucratic variety and others, must satisfy their members' interests and maintain viability. Hence they share the problem of securing adequate feedback to measure their progress toward these goals. In addition, the size and complexity of huge industrial firms may render meaningful and timely feedback impossible. The larger the firm, the more removed is its accounting office from day-to-day operations, and the more difficult it becomes to pinpoint sources of inefficiency. The contributions of particular individuals or departments can hardly be traced in the profits of a large factory. Finally, in industries where oligopolistic conditions prevail, profit bears little relationship to internal efficiency because effective competition is absent. Such industries can remain quite inefficient provided that revenues exceed costs. Only in a perverse sense do the balance sheets of oligopolies reflect efficiency—their efficiency in extracting considerable sums of money from the buying public.

Despite the ambiguous meaning of efficiency and the difficulties organizations face in securing information about their performance, methods have been devised to improve the feedback available to managers. We should review some recent advances in administrative techniques, among which are procedures for the definition of goals, reorganization into autonomous units, and use of performance criteria.

Definition of Goals

Most theorists distinguish formal organizations from other types of social organization. Formal organizations are said to have explicit goals or objectives, often stated in writing, which other forms of social organization lack. We have already noted that bureaucracies as well as profit-oriented firms have multiple goals. While it is true that all formal organizations have objectives, many such goals are stated only in general and imprecise ways, and their relevance for day-to-day activities is not always clear. Public bureaucracies in particular are characterized by uncertain and sometimes conflicting goals. To cite a familiar example, the U.S. Department of Agriculture has one agency, the Soil Conservation Service, that aids farmers in reclaiming land for production, while at the same time the department's Soil Bank Program pays farmers to take land out of production.

When organizational objectives are uncertain, there is a tendency to determine goals and activities according to the resources available. As a high government official has remarked, goals were once determined by "starting with a budget and sending it off in search of a program."[5] Funds were allocated for personnel costs, materials, overhead support, and the like; no attempt was made to link expenditures with objectives. Meaningful feedback is nearly impossible to obtain in this situation; if a bureaucracy does not know or cannot articulate its objectives, it can hardly ask how efficiently it is accomplishing them.

Only recently have government agencies begun systematically to define their long-range goals and programs. The administrative changes which have taken place in the federal government, and first in the Department of Defense, primarily involve definition of goals. The terms "systems analysis" and "cost-benefit analysis" should not obscure the most important innovation, which has been the specification of objectives in a series of programs. In the Department of Defense, for example, three of nine major programs involve the maintenance of strategic retaliatory forces (for the most part, bombers and missiles), continental defense forces, and general-purpose forces to be used in operations short of

[5] David Novick, "The Department of Defense," in D. Novick (ed.), *Program Budgeting* (Cambridge: Harvard University Press, 1965), p. 97.

nuclear war. For each of these programs the department tries to find what level of military effectiveness is required: how much retaliatory capacity is needed, how much capacity to defend the United States, how much capacity to wage limited war, and so forth. An attempt is made to choose weapons that assure the required capacity at least cost. For example, manned bombers, land-based missiles, and submarine-based missiles are considered retaliatory weapons. Should submarine-based missiles be found the least costly way of maintaining retaliatory capacity, the number of manned bombers and land-based missiles would not be increased. Prior to the development of these defense programs, there was no basis on which to choose among weapons systems. The Navy had had its own budget (and submarines), as did the Air Force (with its land-based missiles).[6] Competition and duplication of effort among the services were common. The result of the failure to define objectives was needless expenditure in some areas and lack of capability in others.[7]

Presumably, as other government agencies adopt program budgeting techniques, they too will be able to focus on objectives and reduce needless duplication and other wasteful practices.

Organization into Self-Contained Units

Once goals are defined, there is the question of how to allocate work among the parts of an organization. Classical

[6] *Ibid.*, pp. 86–91.
[7] This discussion of organizational practices in the Department of Defense does not imply that the authors support current defense policies. Nor can we be sure that the administrative changes initiated by former Secretary of Defense Robert S. McNamara have been continued by the new officials in the Department of Defense. It is possible that had cost-benefit analysis been applied to the United States intervention in Vietnam, our troops would never have been sent there. Some political analysts, in fact, argued that the involvement in Vietnam was a result of the failure to define precise policy objectives in Southeast Asia.

administrative theory recognized the distinction between division of labor among departments by purpose, by process, by client, and by place.[8] The first two are the most important and need explanation. Where specialization is by purpose, each unit of an organization has responsibility for making a completed product which is different from products made by other units. In the automobile industry, for instance, there might be one plant manufacturing passenger cars and another making trucks. Process specialization would entail a very different pattern of production. One plant would make the chassis, another bodies, a third motors, and a fourth would assemble them. Classical theory did not indicate what conditions are most favorable to specialization by purpose or by process.

The notions of purpose and process specialization have largely disappeared from contemporary theories of organization, but nearly equivalent terms have been substituted for them. What is called organization by function is similar to division of labor by process. Major activities of an organization are identified—in industry they might be production, sales, and research—and one of them is assigned to each unit of the organization. This functional pattern of organization was used by most industrial firms through the 1920s. With few exceptions, tables of organization showed manufacturing, selling, accounting, treasury, and legal divisions, or variations of these names. Figure 1 shows the organizational structure of the General Electric Company in 1892, which illustrates the functional pattern of organization.[9] The main advantage of division of work by function is that economies of scale can be realized very quickly. By concentrating all manufacturing within one plant, workers

---

[8] See Luther Gulick, "Notes on the Theory of Organization," in Luther Gulick and L. Urwick (eds.), *Papers on the Science of Administration* (New York: Institute of Public Administration, 1937), pp. 1–46.

[9] Figures 1 and 2 are excerpted from W. Lloyd Warner, *et. al.*, *The Emergent American Society* (New Haven: Yale University Press, 1967), Vol. I, pp. 162, 166. By permission.

can be highly specialized. The same holds for the sales force. With only one sales staff, each member is assigned to only a few customers and can become familiar with them. The efficiencies of functional organization do not explain its persistence, however. Often it is unwillingness to change or neglect of administrative matters that sustains an organizational form that was ideal for a simpler firm, even though growth and increased complexity have rendered it inefficient.

The disadvantage of organization by function is that it creates strong *interdependence* between subunits. To use the example of an industrial firm again, sales can sell only what production produces, and accounting must contend with both. Interdependence among units makes their performances difficult to assess. The sales division may generate more revenue this year than last—ordinarily this is a favorable indication of performance—but in so doing it may cause an even greater increase in expenditures for production because of the costs of overtime, premium prices for materials in short supply, or the cost of new equipment. Similarly, if production assembles a large number of pieces at a low per unit cost—again, ordinarily a favorable indication—and if these goods cannot be sold, then the firm's profitability suffers. The economies of scale which result from functional organization must be weighed against the cost of not being able to evaluate accurately the performance of organizational units. In very large organizations, subunits are large enough to realize economies of scale, and the problems of interdependence and of accurate assessment of performance are especially severe. Thus, large size reduces the advantages and enhances the disadvantages of organization by function.

The alternative to functional organization is the arrangement of work into self-contained units. Self-containment means that each unit of an organization makes a contribution to organizational goals *independently* of all others; it is similar to specialization by purpose. In a business organiza-

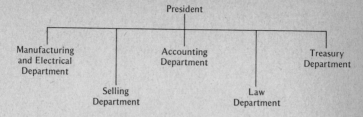

(long vertical hierarchies; up to 20 levels from
President to "workers")

Figure 1. Organization of General Electric, 1892

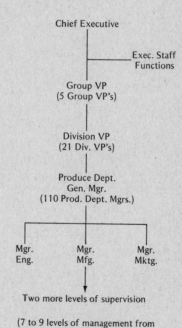

Two more levels of supervision

(7 to 9 levels of management from
Chief Executive to "workers")

Figure 2. Organization of General Electric at Present Time

tion, self-containment leaves each unit responsible for making a product or group of products and showing profit from operations. The current organization chart of the General Electric Company in Figure 2 illustrates self-containment; it shows 5 product groups, which are divided into 21 product divisions, which are in turn divided into 110 product departments. Within each of the 110 departments, production, sales, and research functions are carried out. Each product department buys raw materials and manufactures and sells finished goods. It also pays overhead charges for items such as using the corporation-wide computer network. A separate account is kept for each department, and a profit (or loss) figure is computed for each. As can be seen in Figure 2, work is divided by function only at the fifth level of the hierarchy. Where units are not self-contained (as in Figure 1), work is divided by function at the second level. Above the fifth level of the hierarchy, there is relatively little interdependence among units at General Electric. A small corporate staff and a few top executives are at the headquarters office, but they exercise only general supervision over the product departments. Little hierarchical control by top management is needed precisely because the groups, divisions, and departments are self-contained. Each manager is expected to make a contribution to profit, and this contribution can be measured and is readily known to the managers themselves as well as to their superiors. Because the performance of departments is so easily measured, top executives can make comparisons and allocate bonuses and promotions to the most effective department managers.

Not all organizations can divide work into self-contained units. Firms making a single product (like steel mills or petroleum refineries) and multiproduct organizations desiring to maintain highly centralized control usually have the functional type of organization. Nonprofit organizations can move toward self-containment of units, but this action first requires that managers have a clear understanding of objectives. In principle, there is no difference between holding business managers responsible for independent contributions to profit and holding managers of public agencies responsible for accomplishing other types of goals such as providing public assistance, fire protection, and the like. However, the contributions public agencies make to their objectives cannot be easily specified. It is difficult to assess how much a fire department kept fire losses down through its effective operations, for example. Self-contained units in public bureaucracies also require managers who have sufficient authority over personnel and resources to accomplish their objectives without having to rely on help from other agencies. Again, this is frequently not the case. A number of public agencies are usually involved in a single project; for instance, highway construction requires the cooperation of the public works department, the police, and sometimes the courts in case property is taken by eminent domain, not to mention the contractor who oversees the job and the public auditors who check on him. Rarely does any one of these agencies have full responsibility for the project and authority over the other agencies. The extent of interdependence among public agencies accounts for what is perceived as slowness and inflexibility in dealing with the public; much of their effort is spent dealing with one another. Interdependence compounds the difficulties of evaluating the performance of these agencies because results can rarely be attributed to the operations of a particular one.

James D. Thompson presents a different and somewhat more theoretical argument for specialization by purpose. In his book *Organizations in Action* he notes that interdependence among individuals or organizational units creates a need for communication and coordination of work. Since communication is costly, it is most rational to group interdependent people or units as close together as possible. The efficient organization, Thompson claims, would confine the most intense interdependence (which he calls "reciprocal" interdependence) to work groups, and intermediate levels of interdependence (called "sequential") to subunits of an organization. *Between* larger units, there would be no interdependence save for the influence of each unit's performance on the overall effectiveness of the organization; Thompson labels this "pooled" interdependence.[10] If only pooled interdependence exists between units, they are by definition self-contained and specialized by purpose. Note that Thompson advocates purpose specialization because it lowers coordination costs. We have already shown that purpose specialization improves the quality of feedback available to the managers. These are the advantages of specialization of units by purpose. Its disadvantages are a reduction in economies of scale and less uniformity in standards and administration. Thus the U.S. Civil Service sets personnel standards for almost all federal agencies, thereby discouraging favoritism and unfair competition and promoting uniform application of merit standards. In private industry as well as in government bureaus, insufficient size and the consequent need to maintain economies of scale are the prime reasons for organizing functionally rather than into self-contained units.

Performance Criteria

Organizations without clear measures of output efficiency nonetheless manage to develop performance criteria. These criteria apply to individual workers or at the most to work groups, but not to the whole organization. Like performance criteria that are directly linked to larger goals, they obviate direct supervision to some extent; the rating system rather than a manager's subjective appraisal tells a worker how well he is doing.

The most commonly used index of performance is a record of the amount of work done. An employment counselor may keep track of the number of placements or referrals he makes; an auditor in a public agency may be evaluated according to the number of vouchers he processes

[10] James D. Thompson, *Organizations in Action* (New York: McGraw-Hill, 1967), pp. 54–61.

and approves or disallows for payment. A difficulty with these rating systems is that they can encourage useless or careless work. Thus, the employment counselor may refer applicants who are clearly unqualified or count as placements cases of clients who are returning to former jobs after layoffs. Similarly, an auditor may attempt to maximize his rating by being more hasty in checking vouchers than he might otherwise be.

Often the budget is used as a means of setting standards in public agencies. A performance budget not only indicates the anticipated expenditures of various departments and bureaus, but it also relates these expenditures to some specific activities or services the agencies perform. Thus, the average cost of replacing street lamps may be indicated in a municipal budget. Should the number of lamps needing replacement be below the estimate for the year, a department head would be expected to spend less than he was allotted in the budget. Should emergencies arise, he would be able to justify his high expenses in terms of services rendered by his department. Performance budgets, like accounts of work done, can be abused. If street lamps are needlessly replaced—or if they are reported as replaced when actually they have not been—the cost of work per unit will appear to be low when in fact it is quite high.

In sum, through definition of goals, reorganization into autonomous units, and development of performance criteria, information that managers have about their organizations is greatly increased. Improved feedback is usually associated with decentralization of control, not centralization, because knowledge of objectives and the standards used in judging performance guide people's conduct much better than a supervisor's orders can.

The Impact of Technological Advances

A number of technological advances have occurred in organizations recently; one of the most important is the widespread adoption of automation and electronic data processing. Automation takes a number of forms. It can mean the use of machines to control other machines—the mechanization of mechanized production. It can make possible a continuous process of technology in which raw materials flow in one end of a factory and a finished product comes out the other end, never having been touched or directly manipulated by workers. Automation also affects office work. The use of electronic data processing equipment increasingly replaces conventional record-keeping and accounting systems, greatly reducing the burden of routine clerical tasks.

There has been considerable speculation about possible adverse effects of automation and other technological advances, little of which has been substantiated by careful investigation. For instance, it has been argued that automation creates unemployment. There is no evidence, however, that this is the case; automation usually does not displace workers, though it does require them to learn new skills. It has also been claimed that automation raises skill level requirements. Again, there is little substance to this assertion. It is true that clerical personnel have to learn how to deal with the computer and that factory workers have to learn how to maintain automated equipment, but overall skill levels seem to be about the same in automated organizations as in others. Finally, it is said that the information-processing capacity of large computers will enable a few men who hold high positions in organizations to control large numbers of subordinates, reversing the trend toward decentralization and increased autonomy for workers. Although this is a possibility, experience to date indicates that automation is associated with decentralized rather than centralized responsibility in organizations. Where executives have been reluctant to adopt automated techniques—as has been the case in many European firms—this is often the result of an unwillingness to share authority with the data-processing experts who inevitably accompany the computer and with middle managers in closer touch with automated operations.

Automation and Nature of Work

Advances in technology have affected work routines by eliminating many tedious and repetitive tasks. Robert Blauner's description of the chemical operator's job in an automated plant is strikingly different from most accounts of blue-collar work.

> Very little of the work of chemical operators is physical or manual despite the blue-collar status of these factory employees. Practically all physical production and materials handling is done by automatic processes, regulated by automatic controls. The work of the chemical operator is to monitor these automatic processes: his tasks include observing dials and gauges, taking readings of temperatures, pressures, and rates of flow; and writing down these readings in log data sheets. Such work is clearly of a non-manual nature.
>
> Workers characterize their jobs as being more "mental" or "visual" than physical. When asked if they do any manual work, they will often say that they turn valves occasionally, an expenditure of energy which is not much greater than the office manager's adjustment of the controls on the office thermostat. On the whole, the operators interviewed like this lack of physical effort, although it was not a major element in their over-all work satisfaction. A few regretted the absence of physical activity. They felt their jobs were becoming too easy and that a man could get soft with too much "push-button stuff." Workers with farm backgrounds seemed more likely to express such opinion.[11]

A number of other studies indicate that automation eliminates the most menial and repetitive work. What is sometimes left unclear is that automation, like any other change introduced into an organization, can be disruptive of in-

[11] Robert Blauner, *Alienation and Freedom* (Chicago: University of Chicago Press, 1964), pp. 132–133. Copyright © 1964 by The University of Chicago Press. By permission.

formal arrangements developed over time which workers value greatly. As machines replace men, fewer stations are needed on a production line and the physical distance between remaining operators is substantially increased. Opportunities for conversation, job trading, or "working up the line" by doing one's job faster than the conveyor belt moves, thus allowing a break every few minutes, all but disappear. Work group cohesion weakens; low morale is reflected in higher rates of absenteeism and turnover and in a general sense of discontent. Another source of strain accompanying automation is uncertainty about the amount of a fair day's work. Work groups usually have output norms which differ from official standards. But where such norms are absent, as they usually are when new equipment is installed, unrelenting pressure from supervisors is perceived, and this cannot be resisted by claiming unfairness because no one knows what is fair. Most of the dislocations caused by automation are temporary, however. After a year or two most workers become adapted and probably would find a return to the old pattern as disruptive as the shift to automation was in the first place.

So-called job enlargement frequently accompanies automation. Programs of job enlargement attempt to replace repetitive work with a variety of tasks which fully utilize the skills and abilities of workers. In part, these programs are initiated in technologically advanced organizations because of a commitment to a "modern" style of operation. At the same time, automation alters the work flow so that it becomes less fractionalized, requiring employees to have more diverse skills. A study by Floyd Mann and Richard Hoffman of two power plants—one automated, the other not—illustrates this point vividly. In the old-fashioned plant, Stand, there were three major operating groups, boiler, turbine, and electrical operations, and a number of job gradations within each. In the new plant, Advance, the boiler and turbine functions were integrated as a result of automation. This meant that only men with knowledge of both boilers and turbines could be employed and that the distinction between boiler and turbine operators could not be maintained. Management decided to train men in electrical switching as well as in boiler and turbine operations. The result was that Advance had only one class of workers, power plant operators. Men whose jobs were "enlarged" because of automation found their work much more satisfying than did their counterparts at Stand.[12]

Automation and Hierarchy

An issue of special interest is the effect automation has on the authority structure. Does the installation of computers reduce or increase the number of managerial levels in the hierarchy? Does it lessen or intensify the status distinctions among employees occupying different hierarchical positions? Does it lead to centralization or decentralization of decision-making? It is not possible to give a definitive answer to these questions, for two reasons. First, technological advances such as automation do not necessarily have the same effects in different types of organizations, although some general implications of automation in various kinds of organizations have been observed. Second, the widespread use of computers is a very recent phenomenon, having largely occurred within the last decade. Tendencies evident today may primarily reflect problems of adjustment and differ markedly from the long-range influences computers will have once more experience has been gained with them.

The introduction of automated equipment in an organization appears to increase the number of managerial levels in the hierarchy. Our own research on several hundred government agencies in the United States arrives at this conclusion, and so does Joan Woodward's research on more than

[12] Floyd C. Mann and L. Richard Hoffman, *Automation and the Worker* (New York: Holt, Rinehart and Winston, 1960), pp. 69–72.

one hundred industrial firms in England. This proliferation of levels in the formal structure, however, does not enhance the significance of hierarchical position and authority for social interaction. On the contrary, it seems to diminish the importance of official status, perhaps because many ranks in the hierarchy reduce the social distance between them. Woodward's research illustrates this. Her aim was to identify the impact of technological development on patterns of organization and managerial practices. The firms were classified into three types on the basis of their technology, which she calls "small batch," "large batch," and "continuous process production"—the latter being the most advanced. The firms with the advanced process technology have not only more levels in the hierarchy than the other firms but also a higher ratio of managers and supervisors and a lower percentage of total costs allocated to wages. Most interesting is the description of how little attention is paid to titles and distinctions between line managers and specialists in firms using continuous process methods.

In process industry, it was extremely difficult to distinguish between executive and advisory responsibility. . . . In some firms the line of command seemed to be disintegrating, executive responsibility being conferred on specialist staff. Eight of the twelve firms in which the status and prestige of the specialist were so high that it was impossible, in practice, to distinguish between advice, service, and control on the one hand, and executive responsibility on the other, were process production firms. In the other process production firms, specialist skills and knowledge were being increasingly incorporated in the line. In these firms as in the unit production firms studied, stress was laid on the importance of the line managers being technically competent. Here, of course, the technical competence required was of a different kind; it was intellectual rather than intuitive and based on qualifications and knowledge rather than on long experience and "know-how." In comparison with the managers in unit production, those employed in process production were young. In one process production firm a hundred of the hundred and twenty managers and supervisors were under thirty-five.[13]

An important question that arises is whether the diminished importance of rank and the easing of boundaries between line and staff are reflected in greater decentralization of managerial responsibilities. An early analysis of automation predicts that it will have the opposite effect of centralizing authority at the level of top management in organizations.[14] The argument is that computers speed the feedback of information to top executives and thereby facilitate the exercise of centralized control even in very large organizations. Although the research evidence is by no means conclusive, what there is indicates that automation promotes decentralization or responsibilities to middle managers, contrary to this argument. The comparison of two power plants by Mann and Hoffman indicates that the influence of foremen relative to that of top management is greater in the automated than in the other firm.[15] The data on forty-six British work organizations by David Hickson and his colleagues reveal an inverse relationship between an advanced, automated technology and the concentration of authority.[16] And research on the fifty-three employment security agencies in the United States also finds that automated operations lead to the decentralization of responsibilities.[17]

Today, so it seems, the introduction of automated facilities tends to foster the decentralization of managerial

[13] Joan Woodward, *Industrial Organization* (London: Oxford University Press, 1965), p. 65.

[14] Harold J. Leavitt and Thomas L. Whisler, "Management in the 1980's," *Harvard Business Review*, 36 (1958), 41–48.

[15] Mann and Hoffman, *op. cit.*, pp. 31, 57, 170.

[16] David J. Hickson, *et al.*, "Operations Technology and Organization Structure," *Administrative Science Quarterly*, 14 (1969), 378–397.

[17] Peter M. Blau, "Decentralization in Bureaucracies," in Mayer N. Zald (ed.), *Power in Organizations* (Nashville: Vanderbilt University Press, 1970), pp. 161–162.

authority. This does not mean, of course, that the prediction that automation may help to centralize managerial control will not prove correct at some future date. This prediction rests on the assumption that computers are used for information feedback and managerial planning, while such a sophisticated use of computers in management is rare nowadays. Although computers still serve mostly as an efficient substitute for routine manual and clerical work, case studies of firms in which computers are utilized for managerial purposes suggest that doing so sharply reduces the time required for making managerial decisions. Of course, there is often a great reluctance to institute automated management information systems for fear of its possible consequences. When more experience with computers has been accumulated and the apprehensions about their use in management have been overcome, the trend of the future may be the extensive employment of automated information systems for managerial planning, which may increase centralization of authority in organizations. On the other hand, automated information systems may be utilized to channel more information to middle managers to facilitate their decision-making, freeing top management's time for long-range planning; consequently, computers would continue to promote decentralization of managerial responsibilities in the future, just as they do today.

From Command Authority to Impersonal Control

Because Weber's model of bureaucracy has been subjected to a number of criticisms and amendments, it seems appropriate to inquire whether or not the model remains useful as a description or as a conceptual framework for dealing with contemporary and future organizations. In many ways, undoubtedly, bureaucracies will continue to conform to the Weberian model. Division of labor and specialization are if anything becoming more intense; rules, regulations, and organizational codes will continue to proliferate; efficiency will be stressed (if not achieved) no less than before. The extent to which future organizations will rely on hierarchical authority and "strict super- and subordination" as a means of eliciting desired behavior from members is not clear, however. As organizations grow and assume greater complexity, more coordination and authority of some sort is required. But at the same time, pressures both from within and outside bureaucracies discourage the use of old-fashioned authority which rests on commands and rigid discipline.

External forces militate against reliance on strict command authority in modern organizations, and for several reasons. First, at least in the more developed nations, workers are more prosperous than in the past, and they are not so dependent on their superiors as they once were. (This is not to deny the importance of poverty as a social problem; but by almost any measure the number of impoverished people in the United States has declined in the last decades.) It is instructive to note what supervisor-subordinate relationships were like at the beginning of this century, as illustrated by Frederick W. Taylor's description of how he would get a hypothetical worker named Schmidt, to whom "a penny looks about the size of a cartwheel," to load 47 tons of pig iron a day instead of the normal 12 1/2 tons.

> "Schmidt, are you a high-priced man?"
>
> "Vell, I don't know vat you mean."
>
> "Oh yes, you do. What I want to know is whether you are a high-priced man or not."
>
> "Vell, I don't know what you mean."
>
> "Oh, come now, you answer my questions. What I want to find out is whether you are a high-priced man or one of these cheap fellows here. What I want to find out is whether you want to earn $1.85 a day or whether you are satisfied with $1.15, just the same as all those cheap fellows are getting."
>
> "Did I vant $1.85 a day. Vas dot a high-priced man?

Vell, yes, I vas a high-priced man."

"Oh, you're aggravating me. Of course you want $1.85 a day—everyone wants it! You know perfectly well that that has very little to do with your being a high-priced man. For goodness sake, answer my questions, and don't waste any more of my time. Now come over here. You see that pile of pig iron?"

"Yes."

"You see that car?"

"Yes."

"Well, if you are a high-priced man, you will load that pig iron on that car tomorrow for $1.85. Now do wake up and answer my question. Tell me whether you are a high-priced man or not."

"Vell—did I get $1.85 for loading dot pig iron on dot car tomorrow?"

"Yes, of course you do, and you get $1.85 for loading a pile like that every day right through the year. That is what a high-priced man does, and you know it just as well as I do."

"Vell, dot's all right. I could load dot pig iron on the car tomorrow for $1.85, and I get it every day, don't I?"

"Certainly you do—certainly you do."

"Vell, den, I vas a high-priced man."

"Now, hold on, hold on. You know just as well as I do that a high-priced man has to do exactly as he's told from morning to night. You have seen this man here before, haven't you?"

"No, I never saw him."

"Well, if you are a high-priced man, you will do exactly as this man tells you to-morrow, from morning till night. When he tells you to pick up a pig and walk, you pick it up and you walk, and when he tells you to sit down and rest, you sit down. You do that right straight through the day. And what's more, no back talk. Now a high-priced man does just what he's told to do, and no back talk. Do you understand that? When this man tells you to walk, you walk; when he tells you to sit down,

you sit down, and you don't talk back to him. Now you
come on to work here tomorrow morning and I'll know
before night whether you are really a high-priced
man or not."[18]

Aside from the abusive language, which would be un-
acceptable today, it should be noted that the appeal to
Schmidt is based primarily on money—"Of course you
want $1.85 a day—everyone wants it!" Schmidt is asked to
undertake a backbreaking job and do exactly as he is told; a
cash incentive is used to induce him to submit to arbitrary
authority. To be sure, pay incentive schemes are still employed to motivate workers to exert greater effort, but they
no longer serve as the basis for the kind of unconditional
acceptance of authority that Taylor describes.

A second change which has occurred outside organizations is a decline in the acceptance of authority of all sorts.
This process—termed "deauthoritization" by one commen-
tator[19]—is reflected in negative attitudes of young people
toward the government (and, especially, the police), a
weakening of the authority of parents over their children,
and challenges to other institutions and practices which
have been long taken for granted. Blacks no longer accept
unquestioningly an inferior social status; neither do women;
nor do students. It would be impossible to identify all the
sources of this transformation, but one important cause is
undoubtedly the increasing level of education of people in
most of the world, and particularly in this country. Quite
aside from any influences of many years of schooling on
vocational and professional skills, formal education creates
expectations and values that stress the autonomy and dig-
nity of individuals, and it makes people more sophisticated

---

[18] From pp. 44–46 in "The Principles of Scientific Management" from
Scientific Management by Frederick Winslow Taylor. Copyright
1911 by Frederick W. Taylor; renewed, 1939 by Louise M. S.
Taylor. Reprinted by permission of Harper & Row, Publishers.

[19] See Louis Feuer, *The Conflict of Generations* (New York: Basic
Books, 1969).

about social relations and institutions. As a result of the changes in orientation produced by superior education, members of organizations are likely to be less concerned with an employer's wishes or approval, less easily manipulated by authoritarian practices, and more interested in exercising responsibility and discretion in their jobs in order to obtain satisfaction from the work itself.

Within bureaucracies, several developments have challenged the assumption that hierarchical authority exercised through issuing commands is (or ought to be) the primary means through which coordination of work is accomplished. Advances in technology, which we have already discussed, often act as impersonal mechanisms of control, removing authority from hierarchical supervisors. In an automated plant, such as the one described by Blauner, it is the information supplied by the machines themselves, not the foreman, that determines what work must be done. In emergencies, of course, the foreman retains the authority of his office, but otherwise he has no legitimate reason for ordering others about. Besides, increasing specialization, which typically accompanies technological advances, raises questions about the "chain of command."

As workers in an organization become specialized, each of them acquires a distinctive function, and it becomes likely that managers cannot fully understand the work of all the professional specialists who are formally their subordinates. Hierarchical relationships are modified under these conditions. A manager who relies on strict command authority may, out of ignorance, make unreasonable requests of specialized subordinates and then assert the authority of his office in insisting that these requests be fulfilled. His subordinates may in turn deny an unreasonable request (or a reasonable one, if they feel antagonistic to the superior) by asserting their expertness. They, not their boss, understand the intricacies of the job. Where work is highly specialized, then, attempts to assert hierarchical command authority often lead to conflicts between managers who lack expert knowledge and their subordinates. Increasing reliance on specialized experts in organizations, which technological advances often make necessary, and which the rising level of education makes possible, constrains managers to abandon their prerogative of giving orders without explanation and to find other means of exercising leadership.

The decline in authority exercised through a strict chain of commands does not imply that bureaucracies today are democratically governed. There are fundamental differences between bureaucratic and democratic institutions, which will be discussed presently. It suffices to say at this point that administrative control and coordination are essential for bureaucratic organizations. If command authority is diminishing, therefore, the question arises of what replaces it to effect control and coordination. The answer is: impersonal mechanisms of control. One such mechanism is automation, which circumscribes the duties of various operatives. Other impersonal control mechanisms are explicitly formulated codes and procedures—including work specifications, administrative rules, and personnel regulations. Since the formalized procedures as well as the machine technology are understood to be only means toward an end, they are not likely to be sanctified as symbols and turned into ends-in-themselves—not so likely as are the rules surrounding command authority and discipline (think of the symbolic significance saluting superior officers has in the Army). Such technical and administrative procedures, therefore, are subject to challenge, review, and change. The bureaucratic hierarchy becomes a network for channeling information and appeals for review. Thus, managerial authority still exists in the organization, but it is depersonalized, being exercised not so much through issuing commands and close supervision as through designing effective impersonal control systems.

The trend toward depersonalization of authority in organizations is still in its early stages, and one may anticipate that it will progress much further in the future. The grounds for this prediction are that reliance on impersonal control mechanisms rather than command authority is most evident today in those organizations that have the most advanced technology and the most highly skilled personnel, such as research laboratories. One can expect technological progress and rising levels of education to make other organizations in the future more similar to these than they are now. If trained experts perform tasks within the limits set by the technology and the administrative framework, resort to strict command authority is unnecessary and, indeed, must be eschewed lest it interfere with the exercise of discretion in making expert judgments. Competent specialists tend to be consulted by colleagues and superiors, and the resulting greater frequency of social interaction concerning the work contributes to coordination, further reducing the need for commands. These conditions tend to increase work satisfaction, since they give employees much freedom and discretion. Managers exercise less personal control over subordinates by giving them direct orders, but impersonal mechanisms preserve administrative control and coordination. As a matter of fact, the controlling influence management can exercise in this situation may well be greater than that exercised through a chain of command and strict discipline, because the latter are likely to cause resentment and resistance, particularly in a democratic culture.

Whether or not the internal influence of management in organizations has been increasing, it appears that the external power of organizations, and thus of their management, in our society has been expanding. In part, this reflects the concentration of productive capacity in a few corporate giants; large firms are increasing their share of the market at the expense of small ones. It also reflects the character of what John Kenneth Galbraith calls the "technostructure." The open competitive market in which the buyer can act rationally has disappeared, according to Galbraith. Corporations are as much in the business of creating demand as they are involved in making goods. We thus have the strategy of changing the consumer so that he wants the available goods rather than the other way around.[20] Government agencies have not been immune to this process either. There is a tendency to encapsulate controversial policies and programs into slogans such as "Vietnamization" and to recruit support for the slogan without indicating what if any substance lies behind it. The same technology used to market soapsuds can sell slogans and policies and elicit public demand and approbation for them. Thus, while organizations may have lost some of their direct authority over members, they have acquired important indirect control devices not only over their own members but also over the public at large, with the result that bureaucracies have become the major locus of power in modern society.

In emphasizing impersonality, expertness, and efficiency, Weber anticipated some of the developments that are now taking place in bureaucracies. He also stressed the exercise of authority through a chain of command as a prototypical feature of bureaucracy, whereas the trend is, if our conjectures are correct, away from this authoritarian form of control. Perhaps nineteenth-century technology made the most impersonal and efficient method of exercising authority a rigid hierarchical structure in which communication comprised mostly commands and orders from superiors that subordinates were required to obey. But the advanced technology of the twentieth century necessitates information feedback and specialized skills, which are incompatible with an authority structure resting on blind obedience to orders issued through a chain of command. As a result, authority becomes depersonalized, and impersonal mechanisms of control displace old-fashioned discipline and command authority, thereby mitigating one of the least pleasant aspects of work in bureaucracies. Ironically, it seems that while employees have more freedom, organizations have

[20] John Kenneth Galbraith, *The New Industrial State* (Boston: Houghton Mifflin, 1967), especially Chap. 15.

more power in modern society than in former times. In a democracy this creates new problems which were anticipated neither by Weber nor by the neoclassical critics of bureaucracy. Some of these problems will be discussed in the final chapter.

8

Bureaucracy and Democracy

To assess bureaucracy's impact on democratic values, its internal and external consequences must be distinguished. Either we are concerned with the particular structures that are bureaucratically organized and raise the questions of whether this organizing principle is compatible with internal democracy and, if not, whether the bureaucratization of some organizations is nevertheless justified in a democracy; or we are concerned with the society within which numerous bureaucracies exist and raise the questions of whether they threaten its democratic institutions and, if so, how to protect democracy against this threat. Answers to the first two questions will furnish clues for answering the second two.

To Obey or Not to Obey

Bureaucracy's power of control has implications for its own members, on the one hand, and for society at large, on the other. In addition, it has implications for its clients, who constitute a borderline group, being neither fully part of the organization nor completely external to it. People's ambivalent reactions to bureaucratic authority are revealed by an analysis of the accusation of bureaucratic inefficiency and by an experiment on obedience.

The Accusation of "Red Tape"

There is no doubt that bureaucracies sometimes operate inefficiently. When this occurs, however, clients rarely have an opportunity to observe it. Conversely, many bureaucratic practices condemned by clients are not in fact inefficient. For example, being required to fill out lengthy forms in minute detail, including entries that are clearly not pertinent to the particular case, is inconvenient from the standpoint of the client but may be expedient for the bureaucracy. This requirement is more efficient than permitting clients to decide which entries are relevant, since even occasional omissions of pertinent information would interfere with operations. Think of the last time you accused some officials of being so entangled in red tape that they could not work effectively. Did it happen after you had made a careful investigation and obtained evidence that given operating methods were disadvantageous *for the bureaucracy?* More likely, it was *you* who felt disadvantaged by a bureaucratic decision, and you gave vent to your powerless anger by leveling the accusation without knowing whether inefficiency was involved or not. We all do this—it makes us feel better.

The individual client stands helpless before the powerful bureaucracy, awaiting decisions that often vitally affect his interests. Greatly concerned with his case, he sees in it a number of exceptional circumstances that deserve special consideration, but the impersonal bureaucratic machinery disregards these and handles the case simply as one of a general category. Raging against adverse decisions or interminable delays is worse than futile, since it does not sway the impersonal organization and merely emphasizes one's impotence. Frustrated clients can relieve their pent-up aggression, however, in discussions of bureaucratic stupidity and red tape. Although the organization's ruthlessness, not its inefficiency, is the source of their antagonism, clients derive a feeling of superiority over the "blundering bureaucrats" by expressing an apparently disinterested criticism of performance—a criticism that serves as a psychological compensation for being under the bureaucrats' power. To be sure, we are incapable of direct retaliation when the actions of powerful bureaucracies hurt our interests, but we retaliate indirectly by contributing through our opinion and ridicule to the low public esteem of bureaucrats in our society.

Findings of an early survey on attitudes toward bureaucratic red tape conducted more than two decades ago support this interpretation.[1] People who placed a high value on social equality were found to be more critical of red tape than those who did not. If this criticism were based entirely on factual observation, such a difference would probably not exist, since persons without an egalitarian orientation are as likely to have encountered bureaucratic inefficiency as those with one. If severe censure of red tape, on the other hand, is motivated by resentment against bureaucratic power, the reason for the difference becomes apparent: the more a person values equality, the more objectionable is the experience of being subjected to the controlling power of officials. The same principle can account for the finding that criticism of red tape was most pronounced among individuals who were particularly sensitive about their powerless position.

In the same study, "conservatives" were found to attach

---

[1] Alvin W. Gouldner, "Red Tape as a Social Problem," in Robert K. Merton, Ailsa P. Gray, Barbara Hockey, and Hanan C. Selvin (eds.), *Reader in Bureaucracy* (Glencoe, Ill.: Free Press, 1952), pp. 410–418.

more importance to the problem of red tape than "radicals." (Respondents were divided into these two political camps on the basis of their attitudes toward labor unions.) This finding may seem surprising, inasmuch as radicals might be expected to be most eager to condemn the operations of the government and of private bureaucracies. This very fact, however, may explain their lesser inclination to worry about red tape. When a radical comes into conflict with power structures, this confirms his political conviction that existing institutions are unjust and should be changed. His radical ideology supplies a channel of aggression against the existing social system, obviating the need for expressing his aggression in other forms. But when a conservative comes into conflict with power structures, he is in a more difficult position. Since his ideology does not allow him to denounce the government and private enterprise, even when his interests have been injured by their actions, he often seeks to relieve his feelings of frustration through attacks on the administrative machinery and its red tape.

Implicit in the prevalent condemnation of red tape is a significant social consequence of this practice, which can be most clearly seen in totalitarian countries. In the Soviet Union, for instance, criticism of the government and its institutions is strictly prohibited with one notable exception. Sharp criticism of bureaucratic mismanagement and red tape is permitted and, indeed, encouraged, as indicated by its frequent appearance in the government-owned press. The dictatorship, through ruthless suppression and disregard for the public's interests, engenders considerable hostility, which might lead to attempts to overthrow it. Although the nature of government policies rather than lack of efficiency in their administration is the basis of this hostility, the government reduces the danger that the people will rebel by providing an opportunity for them to release aggression in complaints about administrative red tape. But if this scapegoating serves an important function for a totalitarian regime, it is dysfunctional for a democratic society. Fuming against red tape and bureaucratic *methods* serves as a psychological substitute for opposition to bureaucratic *policies* that violate the interests of individuals. The fact that frustration is expressed in accusations of inefficiency rather than in opposition to policies indicates how powerful bureaucracies are.

An Experiment in Obedience

The power of bureaucracies raises a number of questions that social scientists have only begun to consider. Just and equitable treatment of citizens requires complex laws and administrative codes. For these to function, people must give them at least tacit consent, for there would be hardly enough policemen to enforce the law if most people wished to disregard it. A modicum of obedience is thus a necessary condition for democracy. Should a government insist on total obedience, by contrast, democracy would be undermined, for unconditional obedience precludes criticism and dissent, which are the essence of democracy.

Government officials, of course, are not the only persons who exercise authority in our society and expect obedience. Parents assert authority over children; the church acts as a source of moral authority; and the professions maintain authority in their particular area of competence. There is also the authority accorded to science, which is relatively recent in origin, and which has undermined many traditional beliefs, especially religious ones. Although the scientist's authority is different from the official's, there are important similarities between the two. Both administration and science are based on expertness, which makes them legitimate in the modern world. Most people are willing to suspend their judgment and accept certain directions given by officials and scientists. It makes no sense to disobey an administrator's instructions on how to complete a form or a physician's orders concerning one's proper diet. In addition, officials and scientists have a certain charisma, and both derive some authority from their position. The scientist is obeyed to some extent because he is a scientist, just as the bureaucrat is respected because of the office he holds. Charisma allows people who hold authority to exercise it with relatively little resistance in areas where they have no special competence. For example, both officials and scientists in Nazi Germany branded the Jews as inferior and thereby helped to legitimate anti-Semitic government policies.

A few years ago, Stanley Milgram performed a series of experiments to test people's willingness to obey commands to inflict pain on another person. The initial experiments took place at Yale University. Here is Milgram's description of the laboratory procedure and a transcript of an obedient student.

The focus of the study concerns the amount of electric shock a subject is willing to administer to another person when ordered by an experimenter to give the "victim" increasingly more severe punishment. The act of administering shock is set in the context of a learning experiment, ostensibly designed to study the effect of punishment on memory. Aside from the experimenter, one naive subject and one accomplice perform in each session. On arrival each subject is paid $4.50. After a general talk by the experimenter, telling how little scientists know about the effect of punishment on memory, subjects are informed that one member of the pair will serve as teacher and one as learner. A rigged drawing is held so that the naive subject is always the teacher, and the accomplice becomes the learner. The learner is taken to an adjacent room and strapped into an "electric chair."

The naive subject is told that it is his task to teach the learner a list of paired associates, to test him on the list, and to administer punishment whenever the learner errs in the test. Punishment takes the form of electric shock, delivered to the learner by means of a shock generator controlled by the naive subject. The teacher is instructed to increase the intensity of electric shock one step on the generator on each error. The learner, according to plan, provides many wrong answers, so that before long the naive subject must give him the strongest shock on the generator. Increases in shock level are met by increasingly insistent demands from the learner that the experiment be stopped because of the growing discomfort to him. However, in clear terms the experimenter orders the teacher to continue with the procedure in disregard of the learner's protests. *Thus, the naive subject must resolve a conflict between two mutually incompatible demands from the social field. He must continue to follow the orders of the experimenter and shock the learner with increasing severity, or he may refuse to follow the orders of the experimenter and heed the learner's pleas. The experimenter's authority operates not in a free field, but against an ever-mounting countervailing pressures from the person being punished.*

. . .

150 volts delivered. You want me to keep going?

165 volts delivered. That guy is hollering in there. There's a lot of them here. He's liable to have a heart condition. You want me to go?

180 volts delivered. He can't stand it! I'm not going to kill that man in there! You hear him hollering? He's hollering. He can't stand it. What if something happens to him? . . . I'm not going to get that man sick in there. He's hollering in there. You know what I mean? I mean I refuse to take responsibility. He's getting hurt in there. He's in there hollering. Too many left here. Geez, if he gets them wrong. There's too many of them left. I mean who is going to take responsibility if anything happens to that gentleman?

(*The experimenter accepts responsibility.*) All right.

195 volts delivered. You see he's hollering. Hear that. Gee, I don't know. (*The experimenter says: "The experiment requires that you go on."*)—I know it does, sir, but I mean—hugh—he don't know what he's in for. He's up to 195 volts.

210 volts delivered.

225 volts delivered.

240 volts delivered. Aw, no. You mean I've got to keep going up the scale? No sir. I'm not going to kill that man! I'm not going to give him 450 volts!

(*The experimenter says: "The experiment requires that you*

go on.")—I know it does, but that man is hollering in there, sir. . . ."[2]

In the experiments at Yale, 65 percent of the subjects were fully obedient—they increased the shock level to 450 volts. To check whether the prestige of Yale was what induced people to obey when they might not do so in other settings, Milgram repeated the experiments in Bridgeport, Connecticut, using the name "Research Associates of Bridgeport." Although the rate of obedience fell somewhat in this context, it remained substantial—48 percent of subjects delivered the full 450 volt shock. The prestige and legitimacy of Yale University, then, increased subjects' willingness to obey, but not very much. Several of Milgram's other findings are noteworthy. It appears that proximity to the victim substantially decreased the subject's likelihood of obeying the experimenter's instructions. When the victim was placed in another room and could not be heard except through pounding on the wall, two-thirds of the subjects were fully obedient. But when the subject had to force the victim's hand onto what he was told was an electrically charged plate, thirty percent obeyed. Most striking in these experiments was the difficulty of creating conditions in which nearly all subjects would refuse to inflict pain on another human being. The appurtenances of science hold so much legitimacy that people were willing to suspend their judgment and behave in ways that would normally be described as sadistic.

Milgram's findings, of course, do not prove that human beings will torture one another whenever instructed to do so. They do indicate, however, that people are much more compliant than is generally assumed. Rejection of authority, it appears, is much more the exception than the rule. This holds important implications for the way government agencies are run, because it suggests that bureaucracies

[2] Stanley Milgram, "Some Conditions of Obedience and Disobedience to Authority," *Human Relations*, 18 (1965), 59–60, 67. By permission of the publisher.

ought to be less concerned with eliciting obedience from clients and more sensitive to suggestions and disagreements that are voiced.

In the short run, of course, bureaucracies can order people about without stirring dissent. But as we have learned from the recent past, what is at first passive compliance eventually gives rise to feelings of powerlessness which are expressed in disruptive protest. To wait for this to happen is the antithesis of democracy.

Contrasting Principles of Internal Control

Whatever the specific objectives of a bureaucratic organization, its formal purpose can be defined as the effective accomplishment of these objectives. This is true for an army, for example, which is expected to win battles; for a factory, which is expected to produce goods that can be sold for a profit; for an employment agency, which is expected to find jobs for applicants and workers for employers. There is a second type of organization, however, which has no specific objectives but the purpose of furnishing mechanisms for establishing consensus on common objectives; the machinery of a democratic government is of this type. A third type, cited in Chapter 1, consists of organizations designed to supply their members with intrinsic satisfactions either of a spiritual sort, as in a church, or of a secular nature, as in a social club. The following discussion is primarily concerned with the contrast between internal social control in the first two kinds of organization. Internal conditions in the third type, which will not be analyzed here, are more similar to those of the second than to those of the first type.

Efficiency Versus Dissent

If an organization is established for the explicit purpose of realizing specified objectives, it is expected to be governed by the criterion of efficiency. Such an organization oriented toward efficiency—whether or not it attains high efficiency—has been defined as a bureaucracy. According to this definition, the bureaucratic form of organization is fundamentally different from both the democratic and the autocratic forms. Neither the will of the majority nor the personal choice of a ruler or a ruling clique reigns supreme, but the rational judgment of experts does. Although both authoritarian elements and concessions to democratic values are found in bureaucratic structures, efficiency is the ultimate basis for evaluating whether such elements are appropriate. Disciplined obedience in the hierarchy of authority, ideally, is not valued for its own sake, as it is in an autocracy, but is encouraged to the extent to which it contributes to effective coordination and uniform operations. Similarly, while lack of freedom and arbitrary power are inherently opposed in a democracy, the only reason for minimizing them in a bureaucracy is that they inhibit optimum performance. Bureaucratization implies that considerations of efficiency outweigh all others in the formation and development of the organization.

However, if men organize in order to ascertain the ideas that prevail among them and then to agree on common objectives, their purpose requires that the basic principle which governs their action be freedom of dissent. In this type of democratic organization, considerations of efficiency are expected to be subordinated to the central aim of stimulating the free expression of conflicting opinions. Of course, democratic processes are not the most expeditious way of arriving at decisions either for total societies or for limited associations, such as trade unions. But the fact that it would be more efficient for the leader to decide on the objectives to be pursued is irrelevant, since this policy could not possibly accomplish the purpose of determining those objectives that are commonly agreed upon or express the view of the majority. To assure that the majority viewpoint remains supreme, a limitation has to be imposed on the majority itself. It must not stifle the opposition of any minority, however small its numbers or extreme its views, for unless dissenting voices can be heard today, tomorrow's decisions will not be democratic ones.

Bureaucratic and democratic structures can be distinguished, then, on the basis of the dominant organizing principle: efficiency or freedom of dissent. This does not mean that one principle prevails to the exclusion of the other. The distinction between the two bases of organizing is an analytical one, and both kinds of considerations have some influence upon decisions in either type of organization. However, each of the principles is better suited for one purpose rather than another. When people set themselves the task of determining the social objectives that represent the interests of most of them, the crucial problem is to provide an opportunity for all conflicting viewpoints to be heard. In contrast, when the task is the achievement of given social objectives, the essential problem to be solved is to discover the efficient, not the popular, means for doing so.

Democratic values require not only that social goals be determined by majority decision, but also that they be implemented through the most effective methods available—that is, by establishing organizations that are bureaucratically rather than democratically governed. The existence, therefore, of such bureaucracies does not violate democratic values. But these values are threatened by the encroachment of concern with bureaucratic efficiency upon those institutions where freedom of dissent is essential, where the guiding goal is to enable men to arrive at democratic decisions. Thus bureaucratic efficiency is expected to prevail in specialized government agencies, but not in the political arena. Various attempts to suppress radical political opposition in the interest of national security illustrate how efficiency considerations intrude upon freedom of dissent.

Democratic processes are in particular danger of being undermined by bureaucratization in organizations which have the double purpose of deciding on common objectives, on the one hand, and of implementing the decisions, on the other. Political parties are a case in point. Large-scale democracy depends on the existence of opposing parties. They have the function of giving expression to the political beliefs of people and of serving as channels through which the government can be influenced. To fulfill this responsibility, a party must be democratically organized, which means that primaries and other devices are used to assure that the party program reflects the wishes of its adherents. Democratic parties, however, also seek to win elections, which requires an efficient organization. Hence, they tend to be governed by political machines and national committees, primaries being relegated to a relatively inconsequential role. In order to make parties more effective instruments for winning victories, their function of permitting the voters to decide the political platforms between which they will choose at election time is sacrificed.

Incorporated business concerns furnish another illustration of this tendency. A clear distinction exists between the management of a business and the organization of its legal owners as stockholders in a public corporation. According to our laws and to the principles of capitalism, business is presumed to be managed on the basis of efficiency, but the board of directors of the corporation is supposed to be democratically elected by the stockholders. The procedure employed for this purpose actually defeats its intent. Proxies are provided every stockholder, which give him about as much choice in elections as the citizen of a totalitarian nation. He has almost no way of opposing the existing leadership, since usually he can only endorse this group by signing the proxy or not vote at all. (Any one stockholder can attend the annual meetings and voice his opposition, but all stockholders could not possibly do so. There is no stadium large enough to hold the three million people who own shares of the American Telephone and Telegraph Company or the many hundreds of thousands who share the ownership of other large corporations.) In fact, therefore, most public corporations are dominated by a few officials, and the large majority of stockholders, sometimes owning more than 90 percent of the shares, have no influence on management.[3] Only when a faction arises, as occurred among the stockholders of the New York Central Railroad in 1954, are there alternative slates of candidates for directorships from which to choose, and democratic processes are thus temporarily revived.

This case suggests that the perpetuation of democratic processes depends on permanent factions—that is, opposition parties within the organization. The situation in labor unions, in this respect, is little different from that in business corporations. As long as factional strife prevails in a union, its members can throw their support to either side and therefore influence the policies of the organization; once it ceases, they no longer have this power. Factions rarely survive for more than brief periods, however, since the one that gains control typically fortifies its leadership position by suppressing the opposition. Such undemocratic action is often justified by the need of remaining united in the struggle with employers—internal disagreements weaken the union and must be avoided. Implicit in this argument is the assumption that the sole function of a union is to be an efficient instrument for attaining given objectives, such as higher wages, an assumption representing a very narrow conception of unionism. Labor unions are more broadly conceived as organizations that enable workers to have a voice in determining their employment and working conditions. There are various objectives that a union can pursue. Unless its members decide which of these to seek at any given time, the union does not represent their interests. For this purpose, the union must establish a democratic machinery and must protect it against the threat of

[3] Adolf A. Berle, Jr., and Gardiner C. Means, *The Modern Corporation and Private Property* (New York: Macmillan, 1932).

being destroyed for the sake of increased efficiency or strength. Let us examine how one union successfully maintained internal democracy.

A Union with Two Parties

If internal democracy were to incapacitate a union from being an effective bargaining agent, workers could hardly be expected to engage in such luxury. A study by Lipset and his colleagues of the International Typographical Union (ITU) shows, however, that this development is not inevitably the case.[4] The union, which is democratically governed, is a very strong and effective representative of the interests of its members.

The democratic character of the ITU manifests itself in many ways. Most important is the fact that the officials of the international union and of the larger locals are biannually chosen in elections which are not purely symbolic affairs where the membership merely endorses the existing leadership. In many elections in the past—half of those in the New York local, for instance—the incumbent officials have been defeated. Changes in administration were usually accompanied by sharp reversals in union policy. Thus, one administration favored arbitration with employers, whereas the opposition advocated that union demands should be enforced through strikes and adopted a more militant strategy when it was elected. Since the membership of the union was able to choose between such contrasting alternatives, it actually determined policy. Basic changes in union regulations must be endorsed by referendum, and more often than not the proposals of the leadership have been defeated, a further indication of the independent spirit and democratic power of the rank and file.

Probably the main source of internal democracy in the

[4] S. M. Lipset, Martin Trow, and James S. Coleman, *Union Democracy* (Glencoe, Ill.: Free Press, 1956).

ITU is its two-party system, which has been in existence for more than half a century. Institutionalized parties assure that there is always an organized opposition to the leadership and that voters are presented with distinct alternatives, without which democratic decisions in large groups are impossible. Even the referendum is not an effective democratic mechanism in the absence of an opposition party, which is interested in discussing the administration's proposals with the membership and in pointing out their faults. In one-party unions, where such critical discussions are rarely initiated, most members have no basis for opposing intricate proposals of their leadership, and a large majority usually endorses them. In sharp contrast to the situation in the ITU, the membership in one-party unions is not able to use the referendum to curb the power of its leaders.

Opposing parties create the organizational conditions necessary for democratic processes to prevail. Indeed, they do more. It is often held that the apathy of most union members (and of members of other voluntary associations) is an insurmountable obstacle to democratic self-government. When they even fail to attend union meetings, how can they assume responsibility for managing the affairs of the organization? They cannot, of course, in this event. But the important question concerns the reasons for their apathy. In the majority of unions where the leadership makes all significant decisions, meetings are dull, since only routine business is conducted, and there is no incentive for attendance. The existence of an opposition party greatly alters the nature of such gatherings. It forces the leadership to present crucial issues for discussion. Furthermore, the controversies between opposition and incumbent officials transform even discussions of less important topics into interesting contests. The union member is not merely a spectator; he can actively participate in the discussion and has a voice in deciding the contest through his ballot. Parties are anxious to win converts, and once a union member becomes a partisan, he has an additional induce-

ment for attending union meetings. (Lipset and his colleagues show that ITU members who belonged to a party
attended union meetings more regularly than those who did
not.) In these various ways, institutionalized parties lessen
apathy and stimulate interest in union politics, thereby
providing a firm foundation for participation in democratic
self-government.

What were the conditions that enabled the ITU, virtually
alone among American unions, to establish and maintain a
democratic two-party system? One condition was its strong
position in the printing industry. The members of a weak
union usually must devote all their efforts to the struggle
with employers and have little time or energy left for
creating a democratic machinery in their organization. A
second condition that contributed to internal democracy
was that independent local unions of printers had existed for
many years before they joined together and formed the
International Typographical Union in 1850. Several locals
maintained considerable autonomy, and it was the opposition of certain strong locals to the international administration that provided the original impetus for organizing a
formal opposition party at the beginning of this century.
Third, printers enjoy a fairly high income, not much less
than that of their union officials, and they generally like
their work. While union leaders whose status is far superior
to that of the workers under their jurisdiction often view
defeat in election and the necessity to return to work in a
shop as an unbearable calamity, ITU officials do not. The
latter, therefore, are less prone to try to prevent defeat at all
costs, including the cost of sabotaging democratic methods.
Attempts to undermine the two-party system are also discouraged by a fourth condition, namely, that the democratic tradition has become part of the value orientation of
ITU members. Officials are deterred from disregarding
democratic processes, since such conduct would be strongly
resented by the membership and invite defeat at the
elections.

Finally, the members of the ITU have created a large number of voluntary associations within their union, such as athletic organizations, lodges, social clubs, and the like. Printers spend much of their recreational life with other printers, partly because they often work at night and their leisure hours do not coincide with those of most people. These nonpolitical associations of printers promote interest in union politics and participation in democratic self-government on a wide scale. Printers who are unconcerned with the political affairs of the union usually belong to ITU clubs where they come into contact with fellow craftsmen, some of whom are sufficiently interested in union politics to talk about such matters on every occasion, even when bowling or playing cards. In other words, the recreational associations of printers expose apathetic union members to discussions that are likely to stimulate increased concern with the union and the way it is managed. Moreover, the large number of voluntary organizations furnishes an opportunity for many union members to acquire the political skills involved in the administration of a democratic group. These men constitute a pool of experienced democratic administrators, from which the officials of the two parties and the leaders of the union can be drawn. The widespread active participation in both the political and recreational affairs of the ITU sustains the internal democracy that the two-party system makes possible.

A Challenge for Democracy

In conclusion, let us briefly examine some implications of the prevalence of bureaucracies for democratic institutions. Strangely enough, social scientists who advance diametrically opposed theories about the historical development of bureaucratization agree on its effects. One interpretation holds that the proliferation of bureaucracies is the result of modern capitalism. The economic advantages of large-scale production lead to the establishment of huge industrial enterprises and ultimately to monopolization. These powerful private bureaucracies put pressure on the government to safeguard their interests, for example, by enacting protective-tariff laws and setting up the bureaucratic apparatus necessary for enforcing them. Hence, bureaucracy in government as well as in private industry is the product of forces generated by capitalism.[5] Several neoclassical economists, in contrast, attribute the trend toward bureaucratization to the willful effort of governments to interfere with the capitalist economy. If the government assumes the tasks of regulating economic life, it must greatly expand its bureaucratic machinery, disturbing the competitive mechanism of the free market and thereby facilitating the development of monopolies. The emergence of bureaucratic business monopolies as well as of government bureaucracies is the inevitable outcome of the political decision to meddle with free enterprise.[6] The authors who advance these conflicting theses about the historical origins of large-scale bureaucracy, however, are in agreement concerning its consequences. Bureaucratization concentrates power in the hands of a few men and curtails the freedom of individuals that is essential for democracy.[7]

Bureaucracies endanger democratic freedoms, but at the same time they serve important functions in a democratic society that must not be ignored. Thus Weber points out that bureaucratic personnel policies—employment on the basis of technical qualifications—reduce the handicap of

---

[5] See Franz Neumann, *Behemoth* (New York: Oxford University Press, 1942); and Robert A. Brady, *Business as a System of Power* (New York: Columbia University Press, 1943).

[6] See Ludwig Von Mises, *Bureaucracy* (New Haven: Yale University Press, 1946); and Friederich von Hayek, *The Road to Serfdom* (Chicago: University of Chicago Press, 1944).

[7] For a full discussion of the points made in this paragraph and a criticism of the two theories mentioned, see Reinhard Bendix, "Bureaucracy and the Problem of Power," *Public Administration Review*, 5 (1945), 194–209.

underprivileged groups in the competition for jobs. Blacks, for example, have a better chance of being hired when objective criteria rather than personal considerations govern the selection of candidates. Of course, the children of wealthier families, who can more easily afford the education that qualifies them for the most desirable jobs, continue to have a distinct advantage over others. Bureaucratization does not produce complete equality of occupational opportunities. Nevertheless, the fact that it does minimize the direct effects of status privileges, such as noble birth or skin color, constitutes a democratizing influence.

"Equal justice under law" is a fundamental democratic principle. The executive agencies which help to administer the law as well as the courts, according to this principle, must not discriminate against any person or group. Administrative officials who investigate legal violations have to interpret the law as they apply it to specific cases. Their judgment is usually not appealed to the courts and consequently assumes quasi-judicial significance. Unless all investigators interpret a law in the same manner, some persons will be treated more strictly than others. Hence, the decisions of all enforcement agents should be governed by uniform standards and protected against being influenced by personal considerations. This is another way of saying that bureaucratically organized enforcement agencies are necessary for all members of the society to be equal under the law.

Other contributions of bureaucracy have already been discussed. Democratic objectives would be impossible to attain in modern society without bureaucratic organizations to implement them. Thus, once the decision to provide free employment service to the public had been reached through democratic processes, a complex administrative system for this purpose had to be established. Furthermore, the high standard of living we enjoy today depends, in part, on the adoption of efficient bureaucratic methods of organization in private industry. Whereas, in theory, a low standard of living does not inhibit democracy, in actual practice it does. Large parts of the population lose interest in preserving political freedoms if they are preoccupied with finding ways to satisfy their minimum economic wants. Under these conditions, people are least likely to participate in their democratic government (economically deprived persons are, in fact, less prone to exercise their right to vote than others) and most likely to fall prey to demagogues who promise them some relief from their economic misery.

Were it not for the services rendered by bureaucracies for a democratic society, their existence would not pose a dilemma, only a problem. In such a case, the task would still be difficult, but the decision would be clear: to endeavor by all means to abolish bureaucracies, because they have serious dysfunctions for democracy. First of all, bureaucracies create profound inequalities of power. They enable a few individuals, those in control of bureaucratic machinery, to exercise much more influence than others in the society in general and on the government in particular. This huge differential in political and social power violates the democratic principles that sovereignty rests with all and that each citizen has an equal voice.

The prevalence of bureaucracies in a society also undermines democracy in more subtle ways. Lipset suggests that the existence of smaller self-governing bodies, the voluntary associations, is of crucial significance for democracy in the ITU. They provide experience in democratic participation, stimulate concern with the political affairs of the union, and lessen the apathy that often characterizes the members of a large organization, who feel remote from its administration. In a society with more than one thousand times the membership of the ITU, the United States, democratic intermediary organizations would appear to be even more important for self-government in the larger social structure. Tocqueville made this observation over a century ago in his classic work *Democracy in America*. Since his time, however, many formerly democratic organizations have become bureaucratized. We generally no longer govern our voluntary associations: we simply join them, pay our dues, and let experts run them. As a result, we have less and less opportunity for acquiring experiences that are essential for effective participation in democratic government.

A person must be able to communicate his ideas to others if he is to influence public opinion. In a community the size of the United States, however, the individual's voice is lost, and only organized groups have the strength to make themselves heard. By joining democratic organizations and helping to decide their policies, people have a chance to exert some influence on the larger community. The trend toward bureaucratization in all kinds of large organizations blocks this vital source of democratic influence.

The recurrent demonstrations and social movements of students, blacks, and poor people in the 1960s are in large part, as their leaders often stress, rebellions against the bureaucratization of modern life in the United States and in the rest of the Western world. Despite their avowed Marxism, the ideologies of many recent radical movements are more reminiscent of Rousseau than of Marx, with their fierce condemnation of rational organization, their idealization of warm personal relations among brothers and sisters, and their yearning for a more natural and primitive style of life. What these romantic ideologies ignore is that the bureaucratic form of organization, while it threatens democratic institutions in some respects, at the same time makes essential contributions to many democratic objectives in complex contemporary societies. Even if we could turn back the clock of history and abolish bureaucracies, we would be reluctant to do so because of having to surrender the benefits we derive from them. Some authors have concluded that modern society's need for bureaucratic methods spells the inevitable doom of democracy. But why interpret a historical dilemma as a sign of an inescapable fate? Why not consider it a challenge to find ways to avert the impending threat? If we want to utilize efficient bureaucracies, we must find democratic methods of controlling them lest they enslave us.

This is not an easy undertaking. Its accomplishment may well depend on democratic participation on a far wider scale than has ever been known. Perhaps, the challenge posed by bureaucratization can be met only if all citizens are able and motivated to devote a considerable portion of their time and energy to activities in the political life of their communities. Such a suggestion would have been unrealistic a century or two ago, when most men had to spend most of their waking hours making a living. The efficiency of the very bureaucracies against which we should protect democratic institutions, however, has reduced enormously the working week and increased the number of leisure hours people have at their disposal. For the first time in history, therefore, all men, not merely a privileged few, are free, if they choose, to take their duties as democratic citizens seriously. And as the level of popular education is raised, more people are becoming interested in political affairs. Many problems still lie ahead, as we all know. The full realization of democracy in modern society is a gigantic task. But would it not be a pity to give up in despair just when the tools needed for completing it seem to be in our hands?

SELECTED READINGS

Basic source book

MARCH, JAMES G. (ed.). *Handbook of Organizations*. Chicago: Rand McNally, 1965.

A compendium of original articles on organizations ranging from historical to econometric and mathematical approaches. Of particular interest are Stinchcombe's "Social Structure and Organizations," Udy's "The Comparative Analysis of Organizations," and Scott's "Field Methods in the Study of Organizations."

Theories of bureaucracy and organization

BARNARD, CHESTER I. *The Functions of the Executive*. Cambridge: Harvard University Press, 1938.

An analysis of principles of organization in business by a former executive of a large company, who was one of the first to stress the importance of informal organization.

CAPLOW, THEODORE. *Principles of Organization*. New York: Harcourt Brace Jovanovich, 1964.

A theoretical work that tries to encompass the informal work group, entire organizations, and relations between organizations. Four categories—status, integration, values, and achievement—and variants on them form the SIVA scheme, which is central to the analysis.

GERTH, H. H., and C. WRIGHT MILLS (eds.). *From Max Weber: Essays in Sociology*. New York: Oxford University Press, 1946.

Contains the classic essay on bureaucracy as well as essays on discipline, power, and authority which are pertinent to the discussions in this study. The editors provide an introduction to Weber's life and his writings.

MARCH, JAMES G., and HERBERT A. SIMON. *Organizations*. New York: Wiley, 1958.

An attempt to formalize and synthesize diverse approaches to organizations. Chapter 6 offers an alternative to Weber's notion of bureaucratic rationality by asserting that people usually settle for satisfactory, not optimum, performance.

MICHELS, ROBERT. *Political Parties*. Glencoe, Ill.: Free Press, 1949.

There is no reason to agree with Michel's conclusion that democracy is hardly more than a utopian dream, but there are good reasons for reading his incisive analysis of parties and trade unions. Unless we learn to understand why democracy often does not work, how can we learn to make it work better?

SIMON, HERBERT A. *Administrative Behavior*. 2nd ed. New York: Macmillan, 1957.

A stimulating text on the principles of administration, which are viewed as limits of the process of decision-making.

THOMPSON, JAMES D. *Organizations in Action*. New York: McGraw-Hill, 1967.

Thompson considers only "instrumental" organizations and postulates that environmental and technological factors account for the ways organizations are structured and change over time. Most of what follows consists of concepts rather than propositions, but the concepts themselves suggest directions for empirical research.

WEBER, MAX. *The Theory of Social and Economic Organization*, translated by A. M. Henderson and Talcott Parsons. New York: Oxford University Press, 1947.

The typology of authority in this book includes another general discussion of bureaucracy which is not as complete but somewhat more concise and clearer than that in Gerth and Mills, *From Max Weber: Essays in Sociology*.

Case studies of bureaucracies

ABEGGLEN, JAMES C. *The Japanese Factory*. New York: Free Press, 1968.

Abegglen attributes the phenomenal growth of Japanese industry since 1945 to traditional values in the society. Loyalty and a sense of obligation to employers are reciprocated by guaranteed lifetime employment and provision of housing and family allowances. Abegglen's interpretation has been disputed; see Kunio Odaka, "Traditionalism, Democracy in Japanese Industry," *Industrial Relations*, 3 (1963), 95–101.

BLAU, PETER M. *The Dynamics of Bureaucracy*. 2nd ed. Chicago: University of Chicago Press, 1963.

A study of the interpersonal relationships in two government agencies and the analysis of processes of bureaucratic change.

CROZIER, MICHEL. *The Bureaucratic Phenomenon*. Chicago: University of Chicago Press, 1964.

Case studies of a Parisian clerical agency and a government-owned tobacco plant are followed by discussion of historical and cultural content of French bureaucracy. Crozier emphasizes the dysfunctions of covert power relationships in the French bureaucratic system that make orderly planned change impossible.

GOULDNER, ALVIN W. *Patterns of Industrial Bureaucracy*. Glencoe, Ill.: Free Press, 1954.

An empirical study of the forces that engendered bureaucratization and its consequences in an industrial firm.

JANOWITZ, MORRIS. *The Professional Soldier*. New York: Free Press, 1960.

An examination of military organization, military careers, and servicemen. The armed forces, Janowitz observes, are as much affected by technological change as are other organizations.

Increasing numbers of specialists and the decline of the infantry have challenged traditional military conceptions of hierarchy and authority. The first three parts of the book are of greatest interest to students of organizations.

KAUFMAN, HERBERT. *The Forest Ranger*. Baltimore: Johns Hopkins Press, 1960.

A study of the U.S. Forest Service examines how a widely dispersed organization with no direct supervision of operating employees elicits both loyalty and high levels of performance from its members.

LIPSET, S. M., MARTIN TROW, and JAMES S. COLEMAN. *Union Democracy*. Glencoe, Ill.: Free Press, 1956.

Historical and sociological study of both the bureaucratic and democratic features of the International Typographical Union.

ROETHLISBERGER, F. J., and WILLIAM J. DICKSON. *Management and the Worker*. Cambridge: Harvard University Press, 1939.

The famous study of informal organization in a variety of small work groups at the Hawthorne Works of the Western Electric Company.

SELZNICK, PHILIP. *TVA and the Grass Roots*. Berkeley and Los Angeles: University of California Press, 1949.

A study of the way in which initial commitments of an organization to the existing power structure affected its operations in unintended ways, with special emphasis on cooptation.

Comparative studies of organizations

BLAU, PETER M., and RICHARD A. SCHOENHERR. *The Structure of Organizations*. New York: Basic Books, 1971.

A quantitative study of data on the 53 employment security agencies and their 1,201 local offices in the United States used as a basis for developing a theory of formal structure.

CHANDLER, ALFRED. *Strategy and Structure*. Cambridge: MIT Press, 1962.

A historian persuasively argues that organizational structures reflect strategies to solve problems arising from growth and complexity. Case studies of four huge corporations—General Motors, DuPont, Standard Oil, and Sears Roebuck—illustrate the transformation from highly centralized structures to decentralized organizations giving division managers responsibility for profit.

LAWRENCE, PAUL, and JAY LORSCH. *Organization and Environment.* Boston: Division of Research, Graduate School of Business Administration, Harvard University, 1967.

Six plastics firms and two companies each in the food-processing and container industries are intensively studied to assess the effects of a complex environment on organizational structure. Success in coping with the uncertainty engendered by a complex environment requires differentiation and integrative mechanisms commensurate with the level of differentiation.

MEYER, MARSHALL W. *Bureaucratic Structure and Authority.* New York: Harper & Row, 1972.

A study of 254 city, county, and state departments of finance examines how the formal structure of organizations affects the decision-making process.

WOODWARD, JOAN. *Industrial Organization.* London: Oxford University Press, 1965.

Comparative research on 100 British industrial firms and case studies probe the impact of production technology on organizational structure. Woodward's classification of technology—small batch, large batch, and continuous flow production—yields several interesting findings.

INDEX